THE NEW TRADITIONAL

HERITAGE, CRAFTSMANSHIP, AND LOCAL IDENTITY

gestalten

TABLE OF CONTENTS

CRAFTING TOMORROW

Traditions surround us. They come to life through our practices and rituals. They are carried from one generation to the next in the passed-down stories, knowledge, and skills that keep us afloat: things like cooking, sewing, farming, beekeeping, tattooing, building, bathing, and shepherding.

We tend to think that because modern life is less manual, less familial, less spiritual, and less rooted in the harshness of the wild, our traditions are at risk. It's worrying to imagine that the rituals that bind us to our communities and to nature will inevitably vanish with the passing of their very last bearers. But there is reason to be hopeful. A younger generation is demanding the very things that our modern world seems eager to leave behind: knowledge, patience, observation, slowness, care, ingenuity, and community. Whang-od Oggay—the last traditional tattoo artist in the Kalinga region in northern Philippines—decided to ensure the survival of her art for the next generation by teaching her unique craft to her niece. And practices from the past can hold answers for the future. This is especially true at Mater Iniciativa, a project founded by Malena Martínez and her brother Virgilio, the internationally renowned Peruvian chef. In their agricultural and culinary laboratory, they use an ancient technique from the Incas—vertical farming—to create a new culinary culture with a renewed purpose: saving their local agriculture.

Most traditions aren't disappearing so much as they are transforming. Modern blacksmiths continue to hand-forge tools that will last for generations, and have recontextualized their craft as a counterpoint to disposable manufacturing and planned obsolescence. Chefs in northern countries are mixing ancestral and contemporary techniques in order to use scarce local ingredients all year round. On Fogo Island in eastern Canada, contemporary designers and artists are cooperating with traditional fishers to transform their local economy. Communities and individuals around the world are seeking out creative ways to revive and adapt traditions to make them more sustainable.

Traditions are also shifting to account for climate change. In California, winemakers are adapting their methods to minimize the risk of wildfires. In China, beekeepers use human pollination to mitigate the disappearance of bees. In India, agricultural communities are turning to greenhouses, which have proven to be healthier and longer lasting.

The artisans, entrepreneurs, and communities stoking old traditions often bear witness to our most urgent social and environmental challenges. This perspective has led many young professionals to re-engage with their cultures and locales in more meaningful ways. Such is the case with Björn Steinar Jónsson, who left his job at a global tech company to return to Iceland to revive his country's lost practice of geothermal salt production, and of Ji-ae Chae, who quit being a hairdresser in Seoul to join a community of strong-minded free-diving women practising their centuries-old profession off the coast of Jeju.

Embracing tradition doesn't have to mean abstaining from the internet. In fact, online tools have helped catalyze this revival by enabling people to self-organize, to share their stories and pressing issues, and to take part in new conversations. Technology can offer positive means of resistance: the Ogiek—an agrarian community under threat from the Kenyan government—has used social media to draw supporters to its cause.

From Kenya to Korea, from Iceland to Canada, realities and traditions are strikingly different. But practitioners share a common yearning, a common ground. They are part of a movement for a "new traditional." Their ancestors wove and mended the clothes they wore; they built furniture and heirlooms to last; they cultivated and canned foods to provide for their families. Today, these communities firmly grasp onto rituals and knowledge for a different form of survival. To BESIDE, the print magazine and co-editor of this book, traditions not only have the power to reconnect us with one another, keep cultures alive and relevant, and protect our planet—they are our most essential tool to ultimately build a more sustainable future. Tradition can bridge the gap between humans and nature.

THE MOST AUTHENTIC TRADITIONAL TATTOO ARTIST IN THE WORLD

KALINGA REGION, PHILIPPINES

Whang-od Oggay is the last traditional tattoo artist from the old generation in the Kalinga region in the northern Philippines. This internationally acclaimed tattooist has single-handedly ensured the survival of her generation's art for the next generation.

Whang-od Oggay has seen some changes in her time. She's the last of her kind, a tattoo artist, or *mambabatok,* from the elder generation of the Butbut tribe in the Kalinga region of northern Philippines. Now believed to be more than 100 years old (her exact age is unknown, even to her), Oggay first started tattooing when the warriors of her tribe were still going to war with neighboring tribes and returning with the heads of opponents they'd killed. Today, she's one of the most venerated tattoo artists on the planet, and hundreds of people from all over the world swarm her tiny mountaintop village every day, in the hopes of getting inked by a living legend.

Oggay employs a style of tattooing called *batok,* or hand tapping. All tattoos hurt, but this is a uniquely painful method. The ink is made from a simple mixture of ➤

01 Whang-od Oggay sits for a portrait after completing a tattoo.

02 This small shop is the only place in the village where you can buy things like beer, dinner, and snacks.

03 A simple hand-painted sign informs visitors they have come to the right place.

charcoal and water, which is rubbed onto the tip of a thorn plucked from a pomelo tree (the one behind her house in fact), and then vigorously hammered under one's skin using two pieces of bamboo. Oggay draws her design onto one's skin with a piece of straw and then needles it in at a rate of 100 taps per minute. Not everyone can handle it, but those who do are graced with perhaps the most authentic traditional tattoo in the world today.

Oggay herself is a strict traditionalist. Though keen to ensure the survival of her art, she refuses to pass it along to anyone outside her tribe, because she believes that the practitioner must be part of her bloodline. Thus, she has only two pupils, Grace Palicas and Elyang Wigan, both **04** grandnieces of Oggay and both eager to follow in her footsteps.

A woman of immense beauty, Oggay's glittering eyes, confident demeanor, and elegant full-body tattoos convey the strength of her people and the depth of her lived experience. The Kalinga region is a land of thick jungles and layers of rice terraces carved into the mountainsides, but contrary to the natural beauty, the word *Kalinga* means "outlaw": a testament to the region's historic reputation as a place of danger and violence for outsiders. Through centuries of occupations of the Philippines, first by Spain, then the US, and then **05** Japan, the region never fell to the control of colonizers. Whang-od's only romantic partner died during the Japanese occupation of the Philippines—since then, she never married or had children, instead dedicating herself to tattooing.

Though she rarely leaves her small, remote village of Buscalan, Oggay's fame has traveled far and wide. Buscalan received 170,000 visitors in 2016, up from 30,000 in 2010. But the influx of tourists has not always been kind to the village. Litter is a problem, and Oggay doesn't like people invading her personal space to take photos. However, she recognizes that her popularity has created a new economy for her tribe, and helped to ensure the ➤

04 Oggay marks out the design for a tattoo using a straw and a mixture of soot and water.

05 The simple tools of the trade: a tapping stick, a tattooing stick with a pomelo thorn attached, a ceramic bowl for ink, and a plastic washpot.

06 One of the village's traditional stilt houses.

07 Oggay plays with one of the village children.

08 Photos sent by previous visitors to Oggay adorn a wall of the small home in which visitors sleep.

09 Grace finishes the work when Oggay is too tired to continue.

survival of its traditional artwork, so she accepts the compromise.

Oggay's fame doesn't seem to preoccupy her though, nor does she seem to resent the grinding work schedule, tattooing seven days a week from eight in the morning until five at night. Carrying on the tradition is simply too important. "I have a great responsibility. With every tattoo, I am sharing a piece of Kalinga's history and culture with someone new," she has said, and she plans to continue until she loses her eyesight. Then, at last, she'll rest and let others take up the mantle.

08

09

CRAFTING INNOVATION BETWEEN THE LINES

MADRID, SPAIN

The Spanish industrial designer *Alvaro Catalán de Ocón* combines industrial processes with traditional artisanal techniques to take both beyond their limitations and create a green kind of craftsmanship.

Back in 2011, designer Alvaro Catalán de Ocón took part in a project focused on the reuse of PET plastic bottles as a way of addressing the plastic waste issues plaguing the Colombian Amazon. PET, which stands for polyethylene terephthalate, is a form of polyester (just like the clothing fabric) that is extruded or molded into plastic bottles.

"At the time, I was looking for a project in Colombia in order to get to know the country better and to get involved in the crafts community, which is very rich there. My daughter is half Colombian, so I'm linked to the country in that way," says de Ocón.

From an industrial-engineering standpoint, the project was focused on the deep contradiction hidden in each PET bottle—a product with a very short lifespan that takes decades to decompose. By reconsidering the role of the plastic bottle's material, de Ocón was able to merge local weaving techniques with modern lighting, and the PET lamp was born. It is still an ongoing project but it has now spread from Colombia to Chile, Ethiopia, Japan, Australia, Thailand, and Ghana. The PET bottle, a very contemporary lab-manufactured product, is being metamorphosed into something completely new via perhaps one of the most ancient craft techniques found all over the world: baske making.

Combining new and old, the project tries to resolve an ecological issue through a social activation, empowering vulnerable communities of traditional weavers. Most of the time, these weavers move from the country into urban areas, ➤

02

01 Catalán de Ocón's PET lamp project marries industrial lighting with regional textile techniques.

02 Every color combination is left up to the artisan, ensuring that every lampshade is absolutely unique.

many different lampshades as possible, turning this simple form into an anthropological study of materials, patterns, techniques, and cultures.

Industrial designers sometimes tend to keep absolute control of every aspect of their product, yet de Ocón takes a different approach—letting go of the product's final aesthetic almost entirely. As he puts it: "The artisans know much more and have many more resources than we do, so I'd rather detach myself from the final look of the piece, leaving it to the artisan, and concentrate on the concept." In this way, the PET lamp can really be considered a collaborative effort.

While de Ocón's team concentrates on adapting the methods of turning a plastic bottle into a lampshade, the logistics of shipping the product through a stackable design shape, and adapting the package sizes to those of the local post-office boxes, for example, the artisans are free to use their own patterns as they have been for generations. The latter decide the patterns and ➤

where it's hard for them to find a balance between modernity and custom. The plastic bottle of the PET lamp thus metaphorically represents the bond between their contemporary life in the city and the deep cultural heritage they bring with them.

It's important that these products be *used,* and not relegated to items taking up space. According to de Ocón, "Crafts should produce products for everyday use. I believe that the end of local crafts happens when they fall into the souvenir category."

The process behind constructing these objects is fairly straightforward. First, the bottles are cut into strips, which are then run through a traditional circular loom. Every time a new community is involved in the project, de Ocón's team travels to analyze its techniques and rethink how they could be used to produce more versions of the lamp. Artisans are brought together in a creative workshop for about one or two months. De Ocón dreams of combining, in one installation, as

03 De Ocón's studio in Madrid, Spain.

04 A Riad table, which was inspired by traditional tile designs found in places ranging from the Alhambra of Granada to the Great Mosque of Damascus.

03

05

06

05 In the office hangs a range of lampshades from different projects, bringing together a symphony of weaving techniques, materials, and patterns with deep cultural significance.

06 De Ocón's PET lamp has reached communities around the world.

07 The number of different shapes and lack of restrictions placed on local artisans mean the possibilities are endless.

08 De Ocón in his home.

colors according to their cultural heritage. De Ocón believes in trusting expert collaborators while enjoying and valuing any casualties and imperfections.

The PET project is part of a series of ongoing endeavors revolving around the idea of tradition. Preserving them, yes, but also creating new ones in the innovation process. The Riad table is inspired by traditional tile-making techniques, while HOME/OFFICE is an interesting venture combining a classic Eames office chair and *petit-point*, a very old stitching method.

De Ocón's work revives centuries-old practices through modern design objects—because, from his perspective, industrial production is simply an evolution of craft processes. De Ocón explains: "I enjoy being in the borderlines and making it difficult to position my work in any category." Somewhere between traditional and modern, rethinking materials and processes alike and definitely not restricted geographically, that work is in an interstice where all of this progress happens.

FORGING A NEW FUTURE FOR TRADITIONAL METALLURGY FROM RECYCLED MATERIALS

QUEBEC, CANADA

Blacksmith *Mathieu Collette* built Les Forges de Montréal from sheer grit and love for the art. Now he's passing on his indestructible passion for everything that lasts (longer than he will).

Sweat streaming down his forehead, hands blackened and focused, Mathieu Collette repeats an age-old maneuver with a practiced grip: he hits a piece of metal destined to become a tool or decorative object. When he pauses to speak, everything else continues on behind him. The sound of hammers striking the anvil, of metals colliding to take shape—an insistent stroke of regularity beating the passage of time.

In an increasingly dematerialized world, the forge rings true. For Collette, it's the unifying theme that crosses all of history, including his own. At 44 years old, he has loved metal for so long he can't even remember where it all started. His DNA might be the only thing capable of explaining his unshakable enthusiasm: "I used to tell my parents it was pointless for me to go to school, ➤

since I was just going to be a black-smith anyway. They would give me totally puzzled looks."

When he turned 19, Collette left for France to become an apprentice. Four years later, when he came back to Quebec—in 1997—his grandmother showed him some of her genea-logical research. The young man's hunch had suddenly been con-firmed: he descended from a long line of blacksmiths, the Robichons from the Forges du Saint-Maurice.

When he was leaving France, his master André Maltaverne's forge had been razed to the ground "to make room for nice condos." Collette would therefore be the last of three generations of apprentices. Ever since, he has pursued a mission to revive this ancient art. He created the Forges de Montréal, and against

01 Collette's workshop is a living study in contrast.

02 There is a limited time in which to strike while the iron is hot.

03 Collette builds objects meant to last, which stands in contrast to our era of disposability.

all odds, he has made it last. For years, eviction notices hung over his project, where he has invested all his money and hopes, but he's never budged.

In addition to producing his own work, he supervises apprentices and organizes workshops for the general public at 227 Riverside. The forge is lo-cated in an old pumping station found amid the Bonaventure Expressway, grain silos, and the Lachine Canal—the kind of place where even the clang-ing of hammers against iron goes unnoticed.

That's where Collette has forged doors, gates, street lights for Montreal's Notre-Dame Basilica, a magnificent table made of Damascus iron that would earn him a prize, and innumer-able other projects. The same space also serves as a research lab where, surrounded by pliers, maces, awls, sketches, vises, and band sanders, he spends hours trying to reverse en-gineer ancient tools.

In 2015 and 2016, Collette docu-mented, step by step, how to ➤

make the trade axe the French once swapped for furs with the First Nations. "They would send thousands of axe heads that were stamped, minted like coins. They were worth a certain number of furs," explains Collette. This axe could be used to clear the forest, or simply stay alive in it.

The history of the forge goes back even further. It also separated sedentary from nomadic people, Collette says. The Iron Age marked the beginning of settlements—a requirement for the emergence of civilizations. There is a reason why metallurgy holds a special place in the human imagination—from Genesis to Tolkien's *Lord of the Rings,* and all through Greek mythology.

"The forge is the door that brings us back to values like sustainability, eco-responsibility, and buying local. Its mission can reach beyond the making of objects," adds the master blacksmith. By creating things that last, he wants to take a stand against a system that values novelty, disposability, and waste. "We can't keep

getting containers filled with shit—sorry, I mean containers filled with disposable things." Recycling metals allows for a nearly infinite cycle of creation.

Collette is the kind of guy who daydreams about the incredible things he could forge with all the metal available on the planet. "It would take us 400 or 500 years to reuse all of it," he adds. A nice banister made out of the Pont de Québec? Or a knife made out of the Golden Gate Bridge? There's a certain amount of "melting loss" that occurs every time a piece is thrust back into the furnace's internal temperatures. But even those residues could be swept out of the ashes and melted back into iron ingots, the blacksmith's raw material.

Collette's hands create objects that, in the future, will create others—they endure. More than just a manual profession, the forge is, for Collette, a spiritual experience. He cherishes his workshop as a living study in contrasts: the temperature gap between the hearth and the room, the

subdued lighting to avoid overpowering the shining glow of the fire, the stillness of the anvils from which erupt incandescent shards of iron, the barrels of water to cool the burning metal. Working here becomes a form of meditation. "The window for striking the iron while it's hot is very short. I don't have the leisure to think of anything else; I can't dwell on it. The only time is now."

It's all of this—the meaning, the slowness, the close contact with matter—that attracted Collette's "star" pupil, Ivan Savchev, seven years ago. The 29-year-old Montrealer had moved up from mechanic to mechanical-engineering technician and was well on his way to hitting a wall. "I'd lost all motivation. I didn't want to work just to cater to the interests of the Department of Finance, building objects that were only meant to last a few years," says Savchev.

While the master is frankly stirred by the work of his apprentice Savchev, he remains worried: "I might still have about 25 years ➤

04 Collette reverse-engineers traditional tools.

05 Collette knew from childhood that he would take up his family's ancestral occupation.

06 Metal can be recycled almost infinitely.

07 The forge, for Collette, is a site of meditation.

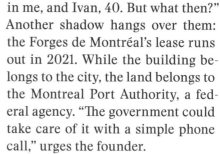

in me, and Ivan, 40. But what then?" Another shadow hangs over them: the Forges de Montréal's lease runs out in 2021. While the building belongs to the city, the land belongs to the Montreal Port Authority, a federal agency. "The government could take care of it with a simple phone call," urges the founder.

Collette "the bad student" has become a jack-of-all-trades teacher when it comes to his passion, and it doesn't stop there. At the Forges de Montréal, he's a spokesperson, adviser, treasurer, director, staff manager, marketing director, intangible heritage specialist, and red tape expert. None of these designations really seem to stick. He's only "doing what needs to be done" to keep the forge going. And he applies the same vigor to his business, his space, and his trade as he does to striking a molten bar of iron.

> Collette's hands create objects that, in the future, will create others— they endure.

08 Collette stokes a fire.

09 Collette's anvil.

10 The coal that fuels the forge.

11 The workshop at rest.

MATHIEU COLLETTE

WEAVING GREENLANDIC IDENTITY

A new generation is breathing fresh life into the tradition of kalaallisut, the national attire of Greenland. Entrepreneurs like *Jeanette Holding* are proud to carry the torch of their ancestor's knowledge.

In Nuuk, the world's northernmost capital, modern architecture embellished with Inuit art stands alongside colonial houses made of wood. These houses sport different colors according to their function, a Danish tradition inherited from the eighteenth century: stores are painted red, hospitals are yellow, police stations are black, and fish plants are blue. Clothing is rather flamboyant. In the streets, young women walk around with cellphones while dressed in brightly colored traditional costumes. The beaded patterns, embroidered flowers, and hand-crocheted lace that adorn their red coats contrast sharply against the immaculate white backdrop of glaciers towering over the city.

Jeanette Holding, the Greenlandic entrepreneur showing us her hometown and roots, explains the reason behind the colorful clothing. "It's the *kalaallisut,* our national costume."

As a child, Holding would go see her grandmother every night and observe her priceless traditional skills at work. "She would always sit in the same place to sew beads, embroidery, or seal pelts. I'd watch her work on the same outfit, piece by piece, for months. It was our quality time." In her family, every woman has a *kalaallisut,* but Holding is the only one who knows how to make and repair them. And she's proud of that. "My grandmother did most of the work and helped make my daughter's and my niece's as well. I'd like to do the same thing for my grandchildren, but I wouldn't tackle an entire costume. It's too time-consuming and really hard on the hands."

While wearing this outfit has become as popular as ever in modern-day Greenland, the art of making it is disappearing as women are progressively shifting away from certain traditional duties to enter the workforce. These days, Holding's education and entrepreneurial career put her in an enviable position—just like her grandmother's skills once did. But back then there was much more to the art than respect and prestige; by skipping back two ➤

28

01 The *kalaallisut*, the national outfit of Greenland, continues to be a source of pride.

02 The colourful architecture of Greenland's capital, Nuuk.

03 The traditional design of the *kalaallisut* is popular with both young and old.

generations, you can see how these women's artisan skills were of paramount importance.

"An entire family's survival could depend on their ability to stitch pelts together into clothing warm enough for the hunter to withstand the arctic cold." But first and foremost, the art of hide tanning had to be mastered. Using a cutting instrument called *ulu*—their most prized possession—women tanned the hides of seals, polar bears, reindeer, dogs, and rabbits. Cleaned, scraped, softened, then chosen according to color, the hides were carefully cut and stitched with the fur facing downward to make sure they kept water out.

Wildlife was used for food, clothing, and even transportation. Pelts covered *qajaqs* (traditional kayaks) and *umiaqs* (small boats with open decks), and no part of the animal went unused—not even the tendons, which were used as thread for making coats. ➤

JEANETTE HOLDING

Apart from being purely practical, clothing also held spiritual significance. It could be used to ward off evil during life's most critical moments: pregnancy, birth, puberty, and death. It had to cater to social and family conventions, but also had to please the spirits of the animals the Greenlanders depended on for survival, so they could be granted their protection in return. For example, the holes in the beads, which were made out of bones, allowed good and evil spirits to "circulate."

In Greenland's pre-Christian traditions, the *kalaallisut* was never worn for special occasions. But, little by little, the women of Greenland saw European celebrations, like marriage, as opportunities to perfect and show off their traditional dress. So they adapted tradition to accommodate a more modern lifestyle.

The nature of the clothing's ornamentation has also adapted considerably. Access to cotton, wool, and silk has made for a much lighter costume. Inuit women have learned embroidery, lacework, crochet, and knitting. The designs that decorate the clothes today are inspired in particular by traditional Danish costumes, a reflection of Danish-governed modern Greenland, where Inuit and European influences intermingle. The beads, which were once made from *ammassat* (capelin) vertebrae, have been made of colored glass since the late nineteenth century. They cover the bulk of a woman's bust and represent her prestige, while the outfit's colors are a sign of her maturity. "Young women wear a bright red shirt under their bead necklace, while older women opt for darker shades," Holding explains. An undeniably effective communication tool, one could say.

The *kalaallisut* is the well-crafted result of Greenland's historical, spiritual, and cultural trajectory, yet it remains unique to every family. "Some of the parts in my daughter's costume were inherited. For example, her bead necklace is the one I received from my aunt, which decorated my *kalaallisut*." Knowing how to repair it not only ensures its longevity—it protects the family tradition.

Those who still know how to stitch together a *kalaallisut* are proud of it, and their skills are becoming extremely valuable on the market. "The outfit can easily fetch 35,000 Danish krone. You save a lot of money by being able to do it yourself."

However, Holding admits that young women are now less inclined to learn how to make it themselves. "I think those who can afford to would rather buy it." On average, it takes nearly 10 years to get a traditionally crafted national costume!

That said, the Inuit continue to find creative ways to integrate traditions into their modern lifestyles. Louise Lynge Berthelsen, a local

Knowing how to repair it not only ensures its longevity— it protects the family tradition.

designer, came up with the idea of starting Nuuk Couture, an environmentally responsible clothing brand that uses natural fibers with a low environmental footprint, such as linen and bamboo. "I'm also the first designer in Greenland to offer a novel version of *avittat* embroidery," she says. Traditionally, *avittat* is made with pieces of seal hides, which are dyed and then cut into small strips and stitched together to create designs. By infusing her traditional expertise with a contemporary approach, Berthelsen is inspiring young women to learn how to make their own embroidery, a trend that can be seen on Instagram and Pinterest.

In a market where quantity too often takes precedence over quality, these young women—following Holding and Berthelsen's example—are instinctively drawn to sustainable and environmentally responsible fashion. Three generations, each in their own way, proudly display the colors of their feminine Greenlandic identity.

04 When she was a child, Holding would watch her grandmother work on the same outfit, piece by piece, for months.

05 Holding holds up one of her *kalaallisut* designs.

06 Holding draws attention to her version of *avittat* embroidery.

JEANETTE HOLDING

LUMBER GAMES

For many of us, the Lumberjack World Championships are just something we catch on TV by accident, but for others, they're a generational tradition with a connection to North America's grandiose and captivating wilderness.

Every summer, men and women of all ages come to the town of Hayward, Wisconsin, in the Chequamegon National Forest toting their handsaws, axes, chainsaws, and climbing spurs. They haven't come in hopes of logging the plentiful white pine; they're here in search of glory at the Lumberjack World Championships. In 2019, 123 competitors from five countries competed in 24 unique categories, such as the Novice Women's Underhand, Men's Single Buck, Standing Chop, Boom Run, and the 90-Foot Climb.

Over three days, roughly 12,000 spectators watched the "Jills" and "Jacks" battle in a festive environment in the Lumberjack Bowl, a natural bowl in the local lake that was once a giant holding pond for the Northern Wisconsin Lumber Company's timber. "It's unique because it's such an authentic event," says Abby Hoeschler, winner of the Boom Run and semifinalist in the Women's Log Rolling. "This sport grew out of a real profession: lumberjacks' desire to have fun and compete while working."

This is true. The history of timber sports is as deep as the roots in this forest. The logging industry in the United States exploded in the mid-1800s. According to historians, between 1850 and 1910, 190 million acres of woodland were cleared for agriculture—at the rate of about 13.5 square miles (22 square kilometers) per day. Many of the trees were also being felled for export, as companies began shipping timber from North America back to Europe, where construction materials were needed. To keep up, companies moved their operations from the East Coast to the Midwest, creating logging camps that provided convenient bunkhouses and dining halls for the men who cleared the forests—better known as lumberjacks.

While chopping and sawing were obvious skills needed for the job, there were other more specialized requirements. "Log rolling talents were perfected in the spring drives as logs were floated downriver from forest to mill," explains Ben Popp, executive director of the Lumberjack »

35

01

02

01 Men and women come to a small town in the Chequamegon National Forest toting their handsaws, axes, chainsaws, and climbing spurs.

02 Logrolling is a test of balance, coordination, agility, and strategy.

03 The lumberjack world championships have become an annual event that attracts tens of thousands.

03

LUMBER GAMES

the annual World Log Rolling Championships—an event that had been moving from city to city." He offered publicity and prize money; he built grandstands of white pine.

In 1960, the championships landed in Hayward. The first year, fewer than 100 fans came out, but by the end of the decade, ABC's *Wide World of Sports* was filming the standing-room-only event.

Today, the Lumberjack World Championships are more popular than ever, but that doesn't mean the competition has lost its small-world senses of tradition, community, or family. Names like Hoeschler, Duffy, Sheer, and Cogar have been generationally represented regulars in the Lumberjack Bowl for decades. Jason Lentz, who hails from Diana, West Virginia, can trace his lumberjacking lineage through 11 generations. His father, Mel, and grandfather, Mervin, are both past champions many times over.

Perhaps one of the sport's greatest appeals is its relative simplicity. Despite the wonders of modern technology, despite athletes in every other sport on Earth streamlining, improving, advancing, and reaching higher heights, very little has changed in the challenges at the core of lumberjack competitions over four generations. "All the events are pretty much still the same," says Lentz. "Just the gear has gotten a little better."

World Championships Foundation. "Only those who possessed courage and had the stamina to stand the long hours, and didn't mind the danger, were selected as 'birlers.' Agile lumberjacks, clad in 'staged' overalls, woolen shirts, and high-topped boots, would ride the logs downriver while pushing, prying, and pulling pike poles to prevent and break up log jams. This workaday birling skill became the sport of log rolling as we know it today."

Eventually, in need of recreation and diversion from the grueling work, and perhaps of an earned sense of gratification, lumberjacks who were driving the logs began to compete against each other to see who was the most agile and quick footed. In the autumn of 1889, the *St. Paul Daily Globe* reported that a "log rolling contest between the lumbermen in the big pool of water at 8 o'clock p.m. will be a most amusing strife and will give Minneapolis people a chance to see a favorite sport of the logging camps." Informal competitions started becoming commonplace at camps across the Midwestern United States.

It wasn't until the 1960s that Hayward local Tony Wise made the Wisconsin town ground zero for timber sports. "Tony was a visionary," says Judy Hoeschler, a former seven-time world Log Rolling champion whose four children, including Abby, all competed. "He called the International Log Rolling Association and put in a bid for

04 Some female competitors—referred to as Lumberjills—are members of Axe Women, an all-women timbersports group.

LUMBER GAMES

THE ENDURING BRILLIANCE OF THE JAPANESE SAP AND LACQUER INDUSTRIES

JOBOJI, JAPAN

Without master sap tapper *Takeo Kudo,* the distinct luster of Japan's home-grown lacquerware might have been dulled to extinction. Luckily, the 65-year veteran shows no sign of laying down his tools.

According to the Ninohe City Council, which promotes the lacquer industry, an astonishing 97 percent of the lacquer used in Japan is imported from China or Korea. Of the remaining 3 percent, produced domestically, 70 percent is produced in the so-called "Urushi Forest" in Joboji, Iwate Prefecture.

Joboji is a tiny inland town with a population of 5,000 that finds itself burdened with the task of ensuring that domestic lacquer production does not disappear. This is because there is no other place in Japan with sufficient urushi trees—a type of sumac—or with the craftspeople capable of properly caring for them and harvesting the lacquer.

The northern prefecture of Iwate has a long history with lacquer, with records showing that the Morioka clan encouraged the planting ➤

of urushi trees as early as the Edo period (1603–1868). But a tree shortage means the urushi industry is facing difficult times. "Right now, there are not enough trees," says Takeo Kudo, a 65-year-veteran of urushi tapping. "It's not just a problem of labor: we can have as many experienced tappers [as there are] in the world but it doesn't mean a thing if there are not enough trees to harvest."

Once planted, urushi trees can take between 10 and 15 years to reach maturity and start to produce lacquer, before which they require constant care. The situation became so dire at one point that the Japanese government stepped in, establishing the Urushi Preservation Society and setting up programs aimed at ensuring the long-term sustainability of the industry.

The tapping season starts around July and ends in October or November, depending on the weather. As much must be harvested as possible within these months, as urushi sap runs slow in the colder months. Takeo Kudo, head of the preservation society, apprenticed to his father, an urushi tapper, and has been doing it ever since. "I started this job right out of middle school," he recalls. "Right after the war there weren't many options in this area. Only one of my classmates went to high school." He says it takes a long time to understand the trees. Over his career he has trained 12 tappers and is considered irreplaceable by the local council.

Urushi sap flows out of the trees and hardens to cover wounds on their surfaces, in much the same way as blood clots. Once exposed to oxygen and humidity, the urushiol compounds in the sap undergo a natural polymerization process to form a hard lacquer nearly impervious to both acid and alkali, and resistant to high temperatures. The urushi trees in Joboji are known for producing sap high in urushiol, leading to a faster-drying and harder lacquer.

In order to access the sap, an urushi tapper uses a unique tool called a *kanna* to scrape a small horizontal line in the bark, then a small blade (a *mesashi*) on the reverse side of the *kanna* is used to make a deeper cut for the urushi to flow out, with a *hera* scraper then used to gather it. This task is actually a lot more nuanced than one may think, with the depth of the *mesashi* cut making a great difference to the quality ➤

01 Urushi tapper Takeo Kudo scrapes bark from a sumac tree to expose a section for tapping.

02 A *hera* is used to scoop up every drop of urushi that flows from the shallow cut made in the tree.

03 This bucket of urushi contains about 50,000 yen worth of product. With so few remaining trees, every drop is precious.

04 Tekiseisha, located near Joboji, exclusively uses urushi harvested in the neighboring forests.

05 Marusan Shikki is a luxury lacquerware company in southern Iwate. Pieces are painted in this sealed room to prevent stray dust and hair getting stuck in the lacquer.

of urushi that flows out. "Each tree can only give a limited amount of urushi, and there is a limited number of trees. Wasting urushi is the last thing we can afford to do," Kudo says.

At present, Joboji's urushi council says there are roughly 142,000 harvestable urushi trees in the Joboji area, yielding a total of 2,750 pounds (1,250 kilograms) of sap in 2018. "We need to produce a baseline of two tonnes a year in order to keep up with demand," says Tetsuya Saito, a worker on the council.

This homegrown urushi is somewhat expensive, but it is used with pride by *shikki* (lacquerware) artisans in Iwate. Joboji's very own workshop, Tekiseisha, is populated by a younger generation of female artisans seeking to preserve domestic lacquerware techniques. The style of coating, which foregrounds the naturally vibrant color and luster of the urushi, is now finding a new audience around the world after almost dying out as a practice.

Further south is the workshop of Marusan Shikki, a lacquerware company founded in 1904. Its style is known as *Hidehira-nuri,* characterized by depictions of nature painted in lacquer and by diamond-shaped gold leaf. It is a complicated process that requires several skilled artisans to work on a single item over several different phases, leading to an expensive final product. Master artisan Takuro Aoyagi says, "It's very difficult and time-consuming to make traditional *Hidehira* vessels, so we've lately begun to release new product lines that have a simpler design philosophy [but] do not lose the essence of what makes *Hidehira* special—a luxurious experience."

The urushi forests surrounding Joboji have benefited from government subsidies supporting the planting of new saplings. Yet it is the hard

06 Marusan Shikki specializes in *Hidehira*-style lacquerware, which is characterized by gold leaf painted in diamond patterns.

07 A Tekiseisha artisan applies urushi using a flat brush called a *hake*. 07

08 Japanese urushi is high in the urushiol compound, meaning it drys and hardens quickly.

09 Although it ends up looking like pottery, Tekiseisha uses carved wood to make its vessels. Here, one is being sanded. 08

09

work of those in Joboji—including Kudo and other tappers, volunteer tree planters, and those on the local council—that is truly what is keeping Japanese lacquer Japanese.

LIFE ON THE CUTTING EDGE

Conceptualizing each knife as a culinary iconoclast, French cutler *Roland Lannier* challenges the traditions and norms around tableware to engage guests in a new dining experience.

Tucked away in his workshop in the medieval city center of Thiers, France, in 2014 cutler Roland Lannier embarked on a pursuit to redefine the knife's role in gastronomic experiences. Characterized by a rapier-thin blade, an unpretentious elegance, and his initials, "L.R.," engraved in a riff on a skull-and-crossbones motif, his knives convey the intriguing values of their maker.

Having worked for over 16 years as a cutler, Lannier noticed that the tableware industry—"l'art de la table"—had been frozen in time for decades, stuck in the heavy influence of art deco. It had faded into the background, offering nothing new to the fine-dining experience. Ingrained in an archaic vision, the field distanced itself from present-day tastes by favoring nonrenewable materials like ivory, horn, and exotic wood. "I wanted to fight against the 'art de la table'—it had all become incredibly bland," explains Lannier. This is what inspired him to work toward a new conception of tableware and redefine the role it plays in the experience of dining.

Despite the persistent stigma that casts the punk movement as a product of aimless and disaffected youth, Lannier has drawn great inspiration from it. As it did for the music world, punk influenced a wide variety of sectors, disrupting social norms and challenging old ways of thinking. "Yves Saint Laurent, followed by Jean-Paul Gaultier—these are people who disrupted their industry by doing things their own way. Today, large corporations are allowing little sparks of madness into their processes because of the punks who carved the path before them," Lannier explains.

It was a spark in the world of gastronomy that inspired the culter to act. Chefs like Ferran Adrià and Yves Camdeborde had already laid the first stepping stones toward a new culinary experience that traveled well beyond the plate. This paved the way for today's great chefs—the likes of René Redzepi, Magnus Nilsson, and James Lowe—to propel the industry into uncharted territories. "Gastronomy today has the power to open new perspectives," opines Lannier. "There are new ways of interacting with guests that allow chefs to cultivate their differences and affirm their own identity. You no longer sit at a table ➤

46

for an experience that is solely found on the plate. Everything that surrounds it must transport you into the chef's universe."

To find his own voice, Lannier revisited the familiar shape of the knife, questioning its efficiency. Each of his pieces is distinguished by an elegant, idiosyncratic design and an unusually sharp blade. Daydream-prone guests risk cutting themselves if their attention should wander, a symbolic statement chosen by Lannier to reposition the knife at the fore of the culinary experience. With the increased awareness comes an opportunity, which Lannier seizes to transmit the values he holds dear by transcribing them into each piece he designs.

From metal shards to Scottish tartan (another homage to the punk world), Lannier detaches himself from the customs of knife making by emphasizing creativity and craftsmanship. Addressing themes like

ROLAND LANNIER

ecology, politics, culture, and religion, Lannier utilizes his access to wealthy guests to prompt reflection and challenge complacency. "Sometimes it's subtle and sometimes not at all. When I conceived the model made from aluminum scraps, it was clearly a homage to the factory worker. I selected a material that evoked filth and impurity, and I placed it in an immaculate and sterile environment, where hygiene is a religion."

No matter the project, Lannier showcases his unique ingenuity.

Recently, he developed a prototype in collaboration with the Michelin-starred restaurant Corner House in Singapore. Inspired by the shift toward zero waste, and to echo the dish with which the knives would be presented, the handle was made from dehydrated onion skins salvaged from the kitchen itself. This touch of thoughtful specificity is what distinguishes Lannier's craft and transforms each of his knives from a tool into a masterpiece.

05

04

01 Roland Lannier and his French bulldog, Leon, sitting on the front steps of his workshop.

02 Rooted in its medieval past, Thiers is recognized as the knife-making capital of the world.

03 In Lannier's workshop, a worker sets nails into a knife handle.

04 The medieval township of Thiers overlooks its modern counterpart.

05 Prototype handle made entirely of dried onion skins from Corner House restaurant in Singapore.

49

REMAKING THE WORLD, ONE GLOBE AT A TIME

How *Peter Bellerby's* London globe-making workshop strives to carry on a tradition that nobody even noticed had gone missing.

Some years ago, Peter Bellerby wanted to offer his father a handmade globe for his eightieth birthday. His father was a naval architect, and such a venerable age called for a special gift. Bellerby's search remained unfruitful for years, having uncovered only either expensive, delicate antiques or poorly made modern globes. Not able to find anyone to make his father one by hand, he decided to do it himself. His project took two years to complete, and almost bankrupted him in the process, but after it was all said and done, Bellerby had found a niche in the market. Not long after, Bellerby & Co, Globemakers was born.

From the time an order is placed, a handmade globe could take months to finish; each must pass through at least five sets of hands before it makes its way to the customer. Everything is customized to order: colors, sizes, the styling of the base, any personalization details. Bellerby's workshop will even add hand-painted illustrations (perhaps of family memories or adventures past) and cartographic additions, like markers on favorite places. Once the map has been designed, it goes to print. Pigments are mixed by hand and the slices of the map get a few washes of color while laid flat, before being expertly wet and stretched across the sphere. It takes an apprentice globe maker at least six months to learn how to properly lay the paper on the smallest-sized sphere and further training is required for each size up. From there, the globe heads back to the painter, and in the meantime the woodworker handcrafts its base. Metal pieces are then engraved and personalized by hand with traditional tools.

According to Bellerby, "there are not many products out there these days that you can personally design to suit your tastes and needs—working directly with the makers and creating something that will hopefully be a family heirloom passed down through generations." Thankfully, people in the digital age are still fascinated by handcrafted objects. A virtual map might help us get somewhere nearby, but a globe will likely inspire us to go somewhere far, far away. "There will always ▶▶

50

01 Hand-painted map strips drying before being placed on a globe.

02 Bellerby globes come in all sizes, but each one is carefully crafted and customized by hand.

03 This kind of work requires high levels of concentration, so all the painters working in the studio must undergo significant training before executing a whole globe on their own.

04 Clients can personalize details and markings on their globe, right down to the exact hue of the ocean.

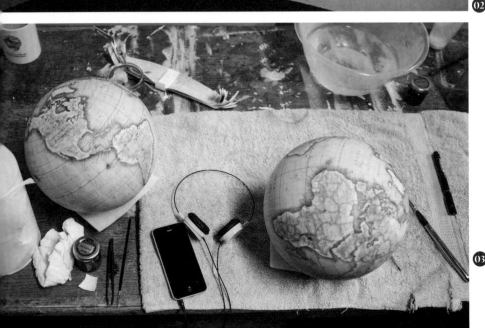

05 Peter Bellerby's team uses techniques and methods he developed himself.

06 Depending on the size, it can take several months to complete a globe.

07 A painter working on a strip of map.

06

be a love for well-crafted items; objects with meaning separate from newer things and progress in the digital world," says Bellerby.

Territories and maps change more frequently than we realize, so Bellerby & Co employs two full-time cartographers to update maps, almost daily. Given the geographical impacts that climate change and political events have on the organization of the world, the company has had to update shrinking lakes and changing polar ice flow, as well as borders of countries that have been remapped. These globes are historical artifacts. They're still timeless objects because, as Bellerby puts it, they're useful historical tools in addition to being generally beautiful objects, ones that should be cherished by future generations, like paintings or sculptures. "There's something amazing about capturing a moment in time on a map—the world as it was during one period," says the craftsman.

The self-taught Peter Bellerby single-handedly created his own tradition. And he is passing it on to his team of 22 engravers, cartographers, woodworkers, metalworkers, painters, and makers. The globe maker has ignited a movement of people eager to master a time-consuming craft.

07

THE FEMALE FREE-DIVERS OF JEJU

When Ji-ae Chae left her career in the city to become a *haenyeo*, she joined a community of strong-minded free-diving women practicing their centuries-old profession off the coast of Jeju.

Four years ago, Ji-ae Chae commuted to her job on the Seoul subway. She spent her days cutting, dyeing, and drying hair at a salon. It was an arduous life: she had trouble finding time to care for her children, she was constantly sick, and interacting with indifferent strangers every day left her drained. Now, like her mother before her, Chae, 33, spends her working days diving into the Korea Strait without an oxygen tank to ➤

gather red sea cucumber, urchins, and abalone from the ocean floor.

Chae is a *haenyeo,* a traditional profession on her home island of Jeju, South Korea. For centuries, female divers have eked out a living by plunging into the sea to gather its edible treasures and sell them. In the 1960s, at the profession's apex, there were 23,000 haenyeo women on Jeju, according to the island's Haenyeo Museum. Now only 4,300 haenyeo remain; many experts believe this generation will be the last,

as young people are fleeing to cities and pollution is destroying the haenyeo's place of work: the fragile aquatic ecosystem of the strait. As of last year, Jeju was home to only 67 haenyeo under the age of 50.

As the haenyeo's numbers have dwindled, interest in them has grown. The aforementioned Haenyeo Museum opened in 2006; in 2015, the Jeju government spent the equivalent of $6.5 (€5.8) million on preservation measures for the haenyeo, such as subsidizing the cost of their

wetsuits and helping to pay for their accident and medical insurance. In 2016, UNESCO awarded the divers a Cultural Heritage of Humanity designation.

No one's quite sure when Jeju's inhabitants first started harvesting shellfish from the ocean floor. Archaeologists have found evidence of shellfish gathering from as far back as 300 BC, while the first historical mention of divers appears in a court document from 1460. These early haenyeo contributed to a shell-trading network with China and Japan. Then, at some point in the 1600s, women started taking over the diving work. This could be because foreign wars drained Jeju's men away from the island; it could be because women's earnings were exempt from the onerous taxes imposed by the Korean king in this era. The haenyeo became exclusively female, a tradition that's endured until today.

Experts say that today's increased interest in the haenyeo stems from the fact that haenyeo is not merely a profession, but a way of life that may soon be lost. ➤

02 Ji-ae Chae kitted out for her day of diving. *Haenyeo* dive with wetsuits, face masks, and flippers—but no oxygen tanks.

02

oceans. Forget danger, forget fluctuating prices, forget modernization—pollution might be the factor that puts an end to the haenyeo once and for all, says Sunoo.

"Years ago when I started interviewing them, they were already saying that the sea underneath wasn't blue or green anymore, and that their products were getting destroyed," she says.

And yet, one of the reasons the haenyeo have received so much respect of late is precisely because of their attention to this destructive force. According to the Jeju Haenyeo Museum, the haenyeo prohibit harvests at certain times to preserve the region's ecology, and they never allow the harvesting of young fish and shellfish. On Chae's side of the island, the haenyeo have collectively decided to catch sea cucumber in the winter, switch to urchins from March through May, and gather seaweed in summer. They don't collect conches in August and September, or abalone in November and December.

"Abalone eat sea trumpet, a kind of seaweed," Chae says. "But because of pollution, the seaweed is disappearing, so the abalone is also disappearing." She adds, "If we can catch the abalone, it's kind of like winning the lottery."

Thanks perhaps to their perseverance in the face of such adversity, the haenyeo have developed a certain flinty and prickly reputation. But Chae, a slight, smiley woman who wears a yellow Disney sweatshirt and a bow in her hair when she's not diving, says that's simply not true. In her experience, the haenyeo are not unlike most women, or, indeed, unlike most people: they love spending time with their friends, they care about their families, they feel pain—despite the fact their work entails diving into the cold ocean until they can't feel their feet.

"Over the past 15 years or so, the respect for the haenyeo has risen," says Brenda Paik Sunoo, a Jeju resident and author of the book *Moon Tides: Jeju Island Grannies of the Sea.* "The haenyeo's legacy is not just economic. It's social, it's cultural."

One cannot simply decide to become a haenyeo and jump into the ocean; instead, the traditional haenyeo culture that so defines Jeju relies heavily on both cooperation and hierarchy. In Chae's village, 13 women currently work as haenyeo, the oldest being 87. These haenyeo are divided into three levels: the bottom level, *hagun,* includes beginners and older women, while the top level, *sanggun,* is comprised of women like Chae's mother, who can dive into the most difficult and treacherous territory.

Chae doesn't shy away from talking about the difficulties of her new life. The haenyeo export most of their products, especially turban snails, to Japan, where they are considered a delicacy. That means, however, that the divers are beholden to the vicissitudes of the international seafood market. They can survive through a combination of diving and farming, but their salaries are not what anyone would call luxurious. A haenyeo can dive from sunrise until lunch, gathering sea urchins, then spend the rest of the day prying them open. For the whole day's work, she would typically make about 17,000 yuan, the equivalent of about $17 (€15).

The sheer amount of time spent under the sea means that the haenyeo have been first-hand witnesses to the environmental devastation of our

THE FEMALE FREE-DIVERS OF JEJU

03

After she finishes diving, Chae removes her mask. She shucks her spoils into a big green bowl; she holds a Japanese flatfish up in front of her face, laughing. It may be a difficult life fraught with dangers, one that might vanish within her lifetime. But for all its flaws, it's the one she's chosen—and she doesn't regret it.

03 Ji-ae Chae holds up abalone she caught that day. Increased pollution means that abalone is becoming rarer in the Korea Strait. Catching one is always a triumph for the haenyeo.

01 The Fogo Island Inn was designed by Newfoundland-born architect Todd Saunders. Newfoundland's original outport settlers were not permitted to build permanent structures, giving rise to a vernacular tradition that used wood instead of stone and placed structures on stilts rather than heavy foundations.

THE NEW ORIGINALS

On a remote island in Newfoundland, makers and artisans have found a new way to use their traditional skills, by collaborating with an international community of contemporary designers.

Craggy and windbeaten, Fogo Island sits perched atop the farthest eastern edge of North America, halfway up the Newfoundland coast. On a map, the small outport island seems to lean into the North Atlantic, like a seabird about to take flight over the ocean. Even in good weather, crashing waves send gusts of salt spray howling inland, and the shoreline never stops crackling with the sound of rocks jostling in the water. No matter where you go on the island, the gray and glinting sea ➤

01

02 Fogo Island is located off the northeast coast of Canada's Newfoundland and Labrador provinces. The island's settlers established their livelihoods by fishing the North Atlantic, and fishing remains Fogo Island's main economic engine.

is always visible: seething, beautiful, and full of promise.

Fogo Islanders have subsisted off the ocean for 400 years, filling their plates and packing their larders with wild game, migrating birds, hand-picked berries, and fresh-caught fish and seafood—a diverse banquet that shifts with the seasons. While commercial fishing and modernization have curbed some of those traditions, if you drive along the coast in autumn, you'll still find large racks of salt cod drying in the sun, and the few restaurants on the island still serve lobster sandwiches and clam chowder from the nearby waters (and even caribou or moose from a local hunter). Roads, meanwhile, are practically a novelty, let alone internet and cell service; old-timers remember when the only way to get to the next town was by boat.

In short, Fogo Island is the last place on Earth you'd expect to find a high-end hotel, not to mention a nexus for some of the freshest and

most exciting contemporary design on the planet. Founded by Zita Cobb, a Fogo native who went on to become one of Canada's most successful tech entrepreneurs, Fogo Island Inn is a graceful white-box construction that cranes out over the rocky shoreline: as light and elegant as folded paper, yet as sturdily suited to the rugged environment as any of the saltbox houses that roost among the island's many bays and inlets. High-profile guests fly in from all over the world to experience the inn's homespun contemporary aesthetic, sustainable ethos, and authentic hospitality.

The organization behind Fogo Island Inn is Shorefast, a Canadian charity created by Cobb and her brothers Alan and Anthony that seeks to "secure a resilient future for Fogo Island" through social-purpose businesses that reinvest all their surpluses back into the community. When Shorefast launched in 2006, the island was in urgent need of revitalization. The local economy had

gone into steep decline in the 1980s, when the collapse of the cod fisheries on Canada's east coast nearly destroyed the islanders' way of life. As more and more people were forced to search for opportunities elsewhere, Fogo Island's vibrant culture seemed to be facing extinction.

The Cobbs believed that the islanders' ingrained inventiveness and self-reliance, and their mastery of traditional skills and crafts could be channeled toward a more prosperous and sustainable future. Along with the inn, Shorefast opened The Workshop, a furniture-building studio that brings together local craftspeople with celebrated designers from all over the world. Especially while the inn was being built, designers like Élaine Fortin of Montreal and Donna Wilson of London were flown in to meet and work with local makers, and to get an inside look at their homes and shops.

These encounters sparked many fruitful collaborations, proving ➤

03

05

04

03 Led by executive chef Jonathan Gushue, the inn's culinary team uses ingredients that have been fished, foraged, farmed, and hunted locally.

04 Mackerel caught by Fogo Island fishers is complemented with mint from a nearby grower and tomatoes from New-foundland's main island.

05 The Shed is a multifunctional space for informal gatherings. Like the inn, it rests lightly on the landscape.

65

06

chair called the "Bertha chair," after Canada's first female Supreme Court justice, Bertha Wilson. The Bertha chair now sits in many of the rooms at the inn, and is upholstered with a specially created lambswool fabric, in a design that Wilson affectionately dubbed "shingle shangle," after a hand-cut wood-shingle pattern that she spotted on one of the Fogo Island homes.

Today, local makers continue to produce the Bertha chair and other products co-created by islanders and international designers. They use the same techniques that they always have, but now they do it for an international market of enthusiastic customers. Despite the changes, the new ethos is very much like the old one. "Life here for hundreds of years was a very independent existence. Everything you did you had to do for yourself, from making your boat to go out fishing to building your house, your furniture, your clothing, your bedding," explains Brewster. "Because everything was being created individually, out of that grows amazing inventiveness." In a local economy revitalized by a social-purpose enterprise, that old-fashioned ingenuity has, at last, recovered its spark and is finding promising new forms of expression.

that the collision of old-fashioned creativity with modern design can produce impressive results. Wilson, for example, picked up on the ubiquitous "barrel chair," a staple piece of furniture in Fogo Island homes. "In the past, everything came in barrels: apples, flour, oil, whiskey—all sorts of different materials that people purchased," explains Kingman Brewster, who heads the design and development team at The Workshop. "The barrel was re-purposed and cut down to be made into a chair. There were many versions; everybody had their own take on it."

Wilson fell in love with the technology of barrel making and joining boards on their edge in order to make a continuous surface. She was also inspired by the traditional boat makers on the island: "I remember visiting the men's outdoor workshops," she recalls. "They all had cozy wood burners and were such a social place, where they would drink beer and build boats." With this in mind, Wilson created a comfortable and contemporary version of the barrel

06 The Punt chair, designed by Elaine Fortin for the Woodshop on Fogo Island, borrows from traditional boat-building techniques.

07 Woodworkers at the Woodshop on Fogo Island handcraft furniture pieces that are products of a partnership between international designers and local makers.

07

08

09

08 Outdoor furniture designed by Ineke Hans.

09 Nick Herder's Puppy table, and a bar stool and dining chairs by Glass Hill.

10 A punt, the workhorse of Fogo Island's traditional inshore fishery, undergoing refurbishment inside Shorefast's heritage restoration project, the Punt Premises.

10

REVIVING AN ANCIENT CEREMONY

After centuries of suppression, traditional Native American practices like the Apache Sunrise Ceremony have seen a resurgence in recent years, as more young people follow the path of their ancestors.

For much of the twentieth century, the ancient Apache tradition of the Sunrise Ceremony lay dormant. A ritual for ushering girls into womanhood, it had been practiced for millennia, long before European settlers arrived in the American West. Colonizers forcibly suppressed the coming-of-age ceremony—along with many other elements of Native ➤

American religion and culture—so that generations of Apache women were unable to make their critical life transition in the way they always had, or were forced to do so in secret. In the last few decades, however, the practice has been recovered. Now, more and more young women are following the path of their ancestors.

Julene Geronimo of the Mescalero Apache Tribe in New Mexico allowed the online magazine *Broadly* to attend her Sunrise Ceremony. The ceremony takes place over four days and entails a lot of hard physical work, such as building teepees and starting fires, as well as rituals of running in four directions. And dancing—lots of dancing. They finish each day with a set of dances, until the last night, when the dancing ccontinues through to dawn. The Sunrise Ceremony concludes with cattail pollen sprinkled on the head of the young woman. Imbued temporarily with the power to confer healing on those who touch her, the whole community eagerly seeks her blessing.

The Sunrise Ceremony is a grueling ordeal, both physically and spiritually. Some Apache women have called it tougher than childbirth. Geronimo made sure to take hers very, seriously, preparing for three years in fact. Her training included learning the songs and dances, athletic cardio in order to get through four days of intense exertion, creating a ceremonial dress, and building a lodge. In the end, it cost her family $10,000 (€9,000)—but it was well worth it. "[The ceremony] will give me a lot of respect as a young lady," Geronimo told *Broadly*. "It makes me very proud that I'm representing my tribe." Besides being a rite of passage for young women, the Sunrise Ceremony draws the community closer together. The cost and effort it takes to do it means that friends and relatives must unite to help out.

Traditional coming-of-age ceremonies are seeing a resurgence despite historic efforts to stamp them out in the not-too-distant past. Before the passing of the American Indian Religious Freedom Act in 1978, various local, state, and federal laws prevented Native Americans from performing spiritual dances and traditional rituals. Through legislation, both the Canadian and American governments sought to eradicate these practices permanently, in order to "civilize" the Indigenous people. Cruel policies were enacted under the pretexts of "education" and "edification." Native Americans sometimes tried to accommodate the imposition of European culture, but European settlers rarely aimed to adjust to the culture of Native Americans.

While Native spiritual and cultural revitalization movements have been active since as early as the eighteenth century, the last few decades have seen an acceleration of Indigenous activism and renewal across North America. This was led by powerful collective movements like Red Power and the American Indian ➤

01 A crown dancer in front of the fire during the all-night dance on the last night of the ceremony.

02 Julene Geronimo, a descendant of the Apache chief Geronimo, on the final night of her rite of passage into womanhood.

03 Geronimo builds a fire by hand the traditional Apache way, one of the many tasks she has to complete during the ceremony.

Movement in the 1960s and 1970s, and today includes the more recent Idle No More movement. Throughout this period, an increasing number of museums have returned sacred and ceremonial objects to the tribes to which they belong, though many such requests by Native Americans have also been denied. The recovery of Native practices has not created a free-for-all; these ceremonies can only be conducted authentically by Native people, and many Native American leaders have come out publicly to oppose non-Native people conducting versions of traditional ceremonies, often done for profit. Nevertheless, some tribes do seek to educate non-Native people about their culture and have made certain ceremonies accessible to journalists and visitors, as Geronimo did for her Sunrise Ceremony.

Although Native spirituality was legally recognized in 1978, the long history of systemic oppression continues to create barriers for Native Americans through generational poverty and hundreds of years of accumulated cultural trauma. Being confined to small reservations and forcibly removed from family and community to be placed in board-ing schools has created deep wounds. But the resilience of Native American tribes and the recovery of their ceremonies have empowered them to rise above the harm that has been perpetrated against them. The revival of these ceremonies may feel bittersweet to the older generations, who were themselves forbidden from performing them growing up, but the joy of seeing their children recover the traditions of their ancestors is a much greater sensation. "A lot more families are going through the rites of passage than before," says Geronimo's grandfather Joe. "They finally get to know that the strength of our people lies within."

The Sunrise Ceremony is a grueling ordeal, both physically and spiritually.

04 Crown dancers act as a form of protection for both the young woman and the community during the ceremony.

05 The teepee is built over the course of the ceremony by the whole community and is used for ritual preparations.

CABALLITO

In contemporary Peru, surfing is a cultural fixture. While surfers from around the world may glorify the region's coastal resources, few are aware of the surfboard's local predecessor, the *caballito de totora*, or "little reed horse."

The *caballito* was created 5,000 years ago in Huanchaco, now a popular beach town in the city of Trujillo in northern Peru. Archaeological findings suggest that it was conceived by fishers from the older pre-Incan civilizations. The curved shape of the craft allowed them to get past breaking waves in order to fish in calmer waters. It was out of necessity ➤

01 Dry reeds being transported from the ecological reserve to Huanchaco harbor, where the bundle will be combined with ropes and foam to assemble the *caballitos*.

02 The old reeds work as fences to shield the young plants from the wind.

03 Carlos "Huevito" Ucañan transporting fresh reeds he cut himself from the ecological reserve.

04 The tall, slender-leaved plant is the perfect material to build watercraft. The reed itself has a hard waterproof shell and a lightweight core, ideal for flotation.

05 Huevito showing young shoots and explaining the root regeneration process. The young plants can be transplanted to a new area to ensure the survival of the species.

that Peruvians learned to surf—a tradition that's survived in the modern age thanks to the initiatives of fishing communities. From one generation to the next, the knowledge of how to build caballitos was passed down, as was an insistence on preserving their raw material: the reed. This sharp plant from the grass family grows in water or marshlands. The swamps located a couple of miles from Huanchaco harbor a large ecological reserve that has been protected by a long line of fishers. Building caballitos involves choosing, cutting, drying, and shaping reeds before assembling them with rope. Each skiff lasts about a month—any longer and the reeds become too heavy and water-logged. This is why the fishers protect their resources from shoreline erosion (a significant issue at present) and drought. The old reeds are used as fences to shield the young plants from the wind, while additional floatation devices, made of blocks of Styrofoam, are removed and put to use in the next caballito.

In Huanchaco, the caballitos are the only kind of boat used to fish along the coast; motorboats are strictly prohibited. The region's young fishers have no choice but to become acquainted with the process if they wish to pursue their trade. Interest in traditional fishing has been on the decline in recent years, and to keep from losing this important part of the local cultural identity, trailblazers like Carlos "Huevito" Ucañan have taken it upon themselves to share the knowledge they inherited. In Huanchaco, beginner fishers and tourists are offered the chance to surf with reed skiffs and are taught how to pick the plants and assemble the crafts. To this day, the activity combines function and recreation, finding deep roots in a community for whom surfing is a mixture of tradition and necessity. ➤ 05

Carlos Antonio Ferrer is a surfer and a Huanchaco native working for the recognition of the history of this sport. In 2012, he spoke about his town to a committee at the nonprofit Save the Waves Coalition, which works to preserve the environmental, cultural, economic, and community-oriented aspects of surf zones, with the goal of creating a World Surf Reserve. As a result, in 2013, Huanchaco became the fifth beach in the world to gain this status. Now a member of the organization's board, Ferrer helps other coastal sites around the country protect waves cherished by the surfing community. Threats such as erosion, industrial development, and urban sprawl can be curbed through better awareness, planning, and community capacity building.

The values of mutual aid, sharing, and respect that go along with wave protection stretch far beyond the borders of Peru. In 2016, Ferrer, Huevito, and surfer Felipe Pomar all took part in a series of enriching encounters on the east coast of Australia. They met with several communities facing the same challenges and were invited to participate in their ancestral rituals as well as to share their own folklore. "Huevito built two caballitos during our trip. The Australian surfers got to try them out," says Ferrer. Created at the dawn of Peruvian civilizations, the caballito is much more than an ancestral sea craft—it's a symbol of intercultural sharing, and of respect for living environments located near and within areas of natural wealth.

CABALLITO

THE KELP AND SHELLFISH FARMER: RESTORATIVE AQUACULTURE FOR THE WIN

NEW YORK, USA

At his non-profit, Greenwave, ocean farmer *Bren Smith* is creating a simple, replicable system that rehabilitates the oceans and could be the answer to growing food sustainably in the face of climate change.

The oceans cover 70 percent of the Earth's surface, but just 2 percent of our food is extracted from them. This is a strong argument in favor of shifting our food production to aquaculture—the rearing of animals or the cultivation of plants underwater—as long as we do it right.

Bren Smith, owner of Thimble Island Ocean Farm, is the executive director of Greenwave, a non-profit that teaches people across the world how to create their own aquaculture farms—a shift away from traditional farming that he has dedicated his life to enacting. Smith's aquaculture model is based on two natural technologies: seaweed and shellfish. Both are naturally regenerative (they do not need feed, fertilizer, or fresh water to grow), filter and clean the ocean water, and can be transformed into biofuels and feed for agriculture. ➤

01 Smith's boat: the key to his vision for sustainable aquaculture.

02 Smith checking his shellfish traps.

03 Shellfish and seaweed are naturally regenerative, filter and clean ocean water, and can be transformed into biofuels and animal feed.

01

02

It's a simple idea in theory, but radical in practice. Unsurprisingly, the man behind it is not your average fisherman—or your average anything, really.

Boats and fishing are in Smith's blood. He grew up in a town called Petty Harbour in Newfoundland, where fishing permeates the culture. At 14, Smith dropped out of high school to work on the ocean—one of the many colorful jobs he would take up, including working as a night janitor in a hospital emergency room, driving a truck, and, on the streets of New York City, selling "wood crap" that he made. In short, in his early years, Smith hustled.

The ocean eventually pulled him back. First, Smith tried to get into aquaculture school in St. John's, Newfoundland. He bought a suit and wore it to his admissions interview. But that didn't work. "You still needed a resumé," Smith says dryly, with his roll-with-the-punches sense of humor. His years of hustling did not equate to an adequate work history for the school.

When an area off Long Island Sound opened its shellfishing grounds for the first time in 150 years, Smith decided to take the plunge and lease space to harvest oysters. "I was terrible at it," he said. Still, he stuck it out and fought his way to oyster farm success. That's what he did—until Hurricanes Irene and Sandy arrived. Smith lost everything and nearly drowned in a herculean effort to save **03** what he could. Like many fishermen from the north, Smith had never learned to swim.

At this juncture, another person might have packed up and moved on. Smith took a different approach: if he was going to make his living on the ocean, he needed a secure model to do it with. That's when Smith found seaweed. "I was learning more about how sensitive oysters were due to climate change and I started looking for other species that, similarly, were also restorative and did not require input," said Smith. "I found Dr. Charles Yarish's world-renowned research on seaweed farming, kelp especially."

Smith had discovered the key to his new project: kelp. "It wasn't just a discovery of kelp," he explains, "it was a discovery of polyculture." What he lacked was a mechanism that would allow him to scale kelp's potential into a sustainable food system disruptor.

At Thimble Island Ocean Farm, Smith has designed a simple yet innovative system of floating scaffolding that allows a particular variety of seaweed called "sugar kelp"—as ➤

building rock-walled clam gardens, as well as from Asian aquaculture, which has cultivated seaweed for centuries, Smith has created a farming practice that is anchored in ancient traditions yet focused on innovation.

This might sound like a business model based on environmentalism rather than taste buds. Most people, when given a choice, want their food to taste good. "My take on this was that, in the climate-change economy, as water and fertilizer prices go up, sea greens and bivalves will be at the center of the plate, with wild fish at the edge. The question is whether this will be delicious or if it will be like force-feeding cod liver oil." There's no shortage of these foods, which are rich in omega-3s and lean proteins, but they're not naturally appetizing. "This is a culinary moment for chefs. Their job is to make disgusting things delicious and beautiful, and if they can't, they should quit their jobs," says Smith.

Is Smith's goal of using sea rather than land for food production, making sure its bounty reaches the greatest number of people in its most delicious form, attainable? He assures me that the interest is there. "There have been requests to start farms from every coastal state and country. This could be the biggest job creator since World War II."

For Smith, oceans are still blank slates. His Greenwave project will continue to work toward its goal of "developing an open-source manual so that anybody can take this up." If we build these systems right—from the bottom up, ensuring that they're poly- and not monocultural, and that low-income earners have access to the products—there is a chance we can push the majority of our food production out to sea.

well as numerous bivalves, like mussels and clams—to grow in both cold and warm climates. "I have a small footprint, but I can grow an incredible amount of food. It's a simple structure and is therefore really replicable. It's the nail salon of the sea: all you need is $20,000 [€18,000], a boat, and 20 acres."

Smith then reminds us that the newest innovations often come from the oldest traditions. "There are two veins in aquaculture: high-input industrial aquaculture that grows what people want to eat—capital-intensive and intensely polluting foods, such as salmon and tuna. Then there's a millennial vein that asks, 'what can the ocean provide and what makes sense to grow?'"

Borrowing from a Coast Salish aquaculture technique that involves

BREN SMITH

04 Boats and fishing are in Smith's blood.

05 Smith uses a Coast Salish aquaculture technique that involves building rock-walled clam gardens.

06 "It wasn't just a discovery of kelp," Smith explained, "it was a discovery of polyculture."

06

85

RESURRECTING THE SALT OF THE EARTH

How *Björn Steinar Jónsson* revived Iceland's lost practice of geothermal salt production

In 2010 Björn Steinar Jónsson was living in Copenhagen and working for a leading global technology company. All around him the city was transforming. Restaurants like Noma were setting new standards for food. The third-wave coffee scene was in full bloom, and a new crop of artisans and craftspeople inspired him to make a major change in his life. Over a cup of coffee with a close friend, he shared an interest in wanting to return home to Iceland to make something to call his own.

Where he landed was Saltverk, a 100 percent carbon neutral salt-harvesting company that harnesses geothermal energy from geysers in the remote Westfjords in Iceland. The idea came from a conversation with Jónsson's close friend Yngvi Eriksson, who was curious about why no one produced salt in Iceland anymore. This led to extensive research and a bold decision from Jónsson to revive the lost tradition.

In Iceland's Westfjords, along the frigid Arctic Ocean, geothermal geyser water maintains a steady temperature of 206 degrees Fahrenheit (97 degrees Celsius); hot enough to boil pristine arctic seawater down to salt. Human interest in this process dates back to the eighteenth century, when the Danes ruled over Iceland. At the time, the king of Denmark had the people of Iceland harvest salt to make *bacalao,* dried and salted Icelandic cod. Fish was, and still is, one of Iceland's most profitable exports, and the Danish king understood how salt played a key role in supporting the lucrative commodity. However, the harsh conditions of the heated saltwater quickly wore out machinery and the upkeep costs were too expensive to justify. Eventually, the Icelandic geothermal salt operations closed in favor of simply importing salt from the Mediterranean.

Today technological advancements like stainless steel make the process of modernizing geothermal salt production more feasible. That said, resurrecting the lost tradition into Jónsson's company, Saltverk, was no easy task. According to Jónsson, "we had no one to look to in how to create the production. Everything was trial and error on a scale of one to one with a lot of failures." Jónsson poured over books about modern salt-making processes in France and Japan that use evaporated seawater techniques for cultivation. From there he adapted this production language to the harnessing of geothermal energy and then set out prototyping equipment. After exhaustive research, rounds of experimentation, and investment in expensive prototypes, Jónsson landed on a model that worked.

To start, pure arctic seawater from the fjord 65 feet (20 meters) away is pumped into the Saltverk facility, a series of unassuming buildings on the shore of Reykjanes, a small town on the northern edge of the Westfjords. Next, the water is boiled down into a concentrated ➤➤

01 Björn Steinar Jónsson harvesting salt from a double-layered pan.

02 The salt works in Reykjanes. The 14,000 cubic-foot (400-cubic-meter) pre-distillation tank where the seawater starts to be distilled is on the far left of the image, with the staff house on the far right. In between the two is the packaging and pan house, where the salt is crystallized before being hand-harvested, dried, and packaged.

02

brine using the geothermal energy of natural hot springs to remove moisture and increase salinity. Once the seawater has evaporated to 15 to 20 percent salinity, the brine concentrate is transferred to salt pans and moved to a secondary facility where it is condensed and distilled even more, to reach 28 percent salinity.

This is the tipping point where salt crystals begin to appear on the surface. When they grow big enough, gravity takes its course and they fall to the bottom of the pan. The pure white salt flakes are then harvested by hand and dried. Finally, the salt is packaged and shipped off to customers. Saltverk's refined process now operates as an almost exact science, creating 22,000 pounds (10,000 kilograms) of salt a week with a zero-carbon footprint.

After the first successful batch was created at Saltverk, Jónsson brought his creation to Gunnar Gíslason, who at the time was the head chef at Dill, the first restaurant to receive a Michelin star in Iceland. The response was far beyond what Jónsson had expected. Gíslason was ➤

03 Chef and restaurateur Christian Puglisi hand-harvesting Icelandic salt during a recent visit to Saltverk.

04 Freshly harvested salt sitting in a draining container before being moved to the drying room.

05 The tank room where new innovations are constantly applied to improve production.

06 Pans 2 and 3 evaporating under natural summer sunlight. This is possible for two months of the year in Iceland. During the winter, the sea salt is able to be harvested under the shimmer of the northern lights.

03

04

BJÖRN STEINAR JÓNSSON

05

06

07

08

ecstatic and urged Jónsson to make as much as possible. Word soon spread and Saltverk built an almost cult-like following. Now, top restaurants and chefs like Matt Orlando, former head chef of Noma, are among Saltverk's loyal and devoted fans.

Despite the steady growth and popularity, the plan for Saltverk's future remains the same as it was from day one. Jónsson has no ambition to build a massive salt company. Instead, he'd rather carefully and thoughtfully nurture the tradition he revived and the brand he's cultivated. Today he only refines the

harvesting process when needed. "We are a flat organization. Everyone here has the title 'Salt Maker.' If my team tells me to fix something or do it differently and they are right, I will change it. Titles aren't helpful—listening is."

Björn Steinar Jónsson continues to breathe new life into the lost tradition of salt making in Iceland and provide pure, natural salt in homes and restaurants globally. This craft may have been forgotten if not for the bold vision of the man who gathers salt at the edge of the world.

07 In the spring, mussels can be found on the shoreline around Saltverk's facilities. An appreciation for food goes hand in hand with being a salt maker.

08 Leftovers from a spring feast at Saltverk: mussels and guillemot eggs served with flaky sea salt.

09 Saltverk's most popular product: pure flaky Icelandic sea salt.

10 Geyser: a geothermal hot spring that bursts when the surface tension of the water hole is disrupted.

11 On the northern edge of the Westfjords, pristine arctic saltwater gathers on the shoreline.

12 Combining the natural hot tubs on the beach with a cold swim in the sea is the perfect end to the day for a salt maker at Saltverk.

09

10

11

FREE-ROAMING MUSTANGS ARE UNDER THREAT—MEET THEIR GUARD-IAN ANGEL

OREGON, USA

The mustang is woven into America's historic fabric, but debates over public land are putting this majestic breed at risk. Through her non-profit Mustangs to the Rescue, *Kate Beardsley* is fighting to protect them.

A native of Michigan, Kate Beardsley moved to Oregon in 1992 to devote her life to all things equine. In 2012, she founded Mustangs to the Rescue, a non-profit that aids unwanted horses and raises awareness about those that have threats looming over them. Today, she is a figure in her community: a strong and compassionate leader whose steadfast convictions are matched by an equally unwavering optimism.

Prior to running the organization, Beardsley trained horses and their riders, with the goal of reaching peak performance. But as the years passed, the overly competitive nature of the business didn't sit well with her values.

"I began to see that the training world revolved around who can make the most money off a horse's back—not what was best for the ➤

animal. I wanted to focus on horses in need, not the ones that had the biggest monetary value," says Beardsley.

The feeling was unshakeable. And so, in 2010, she acquired eight unwanted mustangs, put them to work on her pack string, and found them permanent homes by the fall. With that first cohort came the dawning realization that there are many more horses out there that could be saved, should they benefit from proper training. Today, thanks to local support and volunteer crew members, Beardsley can shelter and **02** tend to upwards of 50 horses, domestic and wild, on the ranch she manages.

Domesticated horses can find themselves in several predicaments from which they require rescuing. Some stories are heartbreaking. For instance, a sick owner who can no longer tend to an animal's basic needs or afford the cost of its upkeep. Other stories tackle a much broader issue: kill buying.

"About 160,000 American horses get slaughtered yearly. The private sector breeds an astronomical number of horses knowing that a majori- **03** ty will be sold to slaughter. A breeder in Oregon will readily admit that he breeds 100 horses to get 1 moneymaker. The 99 others get sent away."

As for feral horses such as mustangs, once a symbol of America's expansive West, they are now entangled in convoluted political quarrels over public land rights and reallocation. In 1971, the US Congress passed the Wild and Free-Roaming Horses and Burros Act to protect and preserve these iconic animals. The act has been disputed ever since, and with the country's current political divisiveness, wild horses have become wild cards.

"It's a very real threat. There's a lot of pressure on public land. When you have several industries—recreation, wildlife, ranching, mining, etcetera—who all have competing interests, horses can seriously lose out. Our law is very clear, but the management never is."

To contain the population of wild horses, whose exact size is disputed, and avoid the overgrazing of public land, the Bureau of Land Management rounds up excess stallions and mares, and moves them to holding pens. Although the bureau promotes the adoption of these displaced horses, federal officials have also contemplated broad-scale euthanasia and mare spaying as containment tactics. ≫

01 "In America, mustangs are legendary. Nevertheless, how we feel may not be reflected in the actions we take."

02 Beardsley trains rescued wild horses and helps them rebuild their confidence.

03 Caught in a politicized limbo, wild horses like mustangs find themselves in a precarious position.

KATE BEARDSLEY

There is something indescribable about the wild horses in the Ochoco Mountains, east of Prineville, that keeps me in Oregon.

specialized in search and rescue or scent detection to help find missing persons. If a scent detection horse seems like a far-fetched idea, it's because of a generalized misconception of what these magnificent animals are actually capable of accomplishing.

"There are plenty of aspects of horsemanship that have been lost. Scent detection, for example, was used for centuries. Not quite in the same context, but [Meriwether] Lewis and [William] Clark used their horses for this purpose. So did Teddy Roosevelt. When he went buffalo hunting, he'd want a horse with a nose. That's a skill **04** that we can currently use, but very few people know it's even possible."

"In America, mustangs are legendary. Nevertheless, how we feel may not be reflected in the actions we take. I believe wild horses have a value the way they are: free. Nature is their best manager."

This is why Beardsley puts domesticated and wild rescued horses to good use. "An animal with training is an animal with a future," she explains. Through rehabilitation, she builds their self-confidence, their trust, and their skills. The approach takes time, but the success stories make it worthwhile. From the hundreds of adoptable horses Beardsley has trained, some have gone on to become excellent backcountry packers; others are

Concluding, Beardsley ponders, "How do you keep sacred things sacred? How do we breed less and care more?" For her and a legion of volunteer ranchers, the answer may reside in the worthwhile investment of restoring lost traditions to create new value, one horse at a time.

04 Even Beardsley's faithful dog helps out with the day's chores.

05 "An animal with training is an animal with a future."

KATE BEARDSLEY

06

06 "I believe wild horses have a value the way they are: free. Nature is their best manager."

07 Beardsley has trained hundreds of adoptable horses.

07

SKI RITUALS

For many people around the world, skiing is not only a sport: it's an ever-evolving tradition that offers a connection to a place, a landscape, and others.

There is no snow in Oukaïmeden, a ski resort in the High Atlas Mountains of Morocco. But sometime after midnight, it begins, and by first light, the mountain is fully cloaked in several feet of white. As daybreak fog lifts, a long line of butter-yellow taxis pulls in from Marrakech. It's not just the rumor of snow that brings people up here; it's the possibility of skiing.

In its most basic form, skiing is the tradition of strapping a long, slender board to each foot with the purpose of sliding over a surface, most often snow. It exists as both pastime and sport, a mode of travel and even, for some, a means to survival. More deeply, it invites us to connect with the surrounding landscape, the ground underfoot, and to the people who share in the experience.

It's not long before the mountainside at Oukaïmeden is dotted with people. Some are leaned over, focused on mastering the art of the snowplow, while others are learning how to walk wearing ski boots for the first time. Some take turns posing with skis, purses in hand, with no real intention of skiing at all, as a few others whimsically throw snowballs into the air. There are those that gaze apprehensively toward the summit, and the ones who have their skis pointed down, determined: ready to push off.

At first glance, this scene shares traits with many other snowy places around the world. From Israel to Canada, Kosovo to India, Morocco to Switzerland—downhill skiing exists almost everywhere snow falls on a slope. Where there is skiing, collective joy can often be found. Big mountains and backroad hills become venues to experience the feeling of giving oneself over to gravity, regardless of location. There is also a sense of freedom in this setting: a moment of being temporarily released of whatever restrictions may be binding one's life. In this way, skiing offers an opportunity to feel the collective flicker of humanness, to share in a moment that transcends personal identity and circumstance.

Despite its modern reputation, skiing was first invented for pragmatic reasons. Essentially, to get around during winter when the snow-covered ground made hunting a challenge. Some of the world's oldest ski artifacts date back to 6000 BC in northern Russia. Here, the tradition of skiing still exists in pockets of the region. In one location, the Kuznetsk Alatau Mountains, skis are handmade from aspen trees and remain an essential travel tool for hunting antelope in the winter months.

Whether skiing is done for pleasure or purpose, to observe it in ➤

01 Visitors enjoy a range of activities at the base of a small ski hill in the Solang Valley, near Manali in India's Himachal Pradesh.

01

02

03

04

05

06

07

situ is to gain insights into the built and natural environments of a place. The food and attire. The languages spoken. The surrounding wilderness. The signage. The scents and sounds carried in the air overhead. The types of trees boughed by snow. The sometimes invisible yet inherently present political backdrop. The dynamics delicately unfolding between strangers, families, friends. All of these distinct fragments combine to make a place what it is; they become part of the place's shared story.

Skiers who return season after season to the same location have the potential to develop time-layered perspectives. Whether aware of it or not, these skiers, by returning, repeatedly engage with place-based phenomena uniquely experienced through the act of skiing: curious birdsong, neighboring industrial activity, glacial retreat, tree growth, weather variances, the amount of snowfall each year. The tradition of annually returning to a place to ski, be it at a mountain hut or an urban ski hill, provides an opportunity to build a long-term relationship with the touchpoints found therein.

At Oukaïmeden the snow is often short lived. By early afternoon the low-elevation layer has evaporated and a herd of goats happily nibble shrubs where, only a few hours earlier, the skiers slid. The absence of snow becomes a constant reminder of its ephemeral beauty, how easily a landscape can be transformed, even if only superficially. Rental skis and boots are packed up and carried by the armload or strapped onto donkeys. As the sun drops, a handful of skiers from Marrakech dip into tajine at one of the few nearby restaurants, an après-ski tradition likely to be shared again.

02 Summit Lake Ski Hill near Nakusp, Canada.

03 Mount Hermon Ski Resort in Israel.

04 Backcountry skiing in Siberia.

05 Homemade skis in Siberia.

06 Palandöken Ski Center in eastern Turkey.

07 Bringing the beach to the slopes.

08 Sand skiing on dunes near Merzouga in Morocco.

09 A tourist from Côte d'Ivoire poses with skis at Oukaïmeden, a ski resort in Morocco's High Atlas Mountains.

10 A ski guide in Gulmarg, Kashmir.

08

09

10

A MODERN FALCONER REVIVES AN ANCIENT ART FORM

The art of falconry has seen a renaissance in recent decades, thanks in part to specialists like *Marc-André Fortin* who've given predator birds a new, counter-intuitive mission: harm-free wildlife management.

Marc-André Fortin has been practicing falconry professionally for 13 years, but don't call what he does a job. For the Montreal-based animal control specialist, it is an art, one that has been practiced for thousands of years. In the last few decades, falconry has seen a major revival, in part because animal control specialists like Fortin have forged a new kind of partnership with the intelligent predators. Falconry today offers a unique natural solution to wildlife overpopulation and habitat management at parks, farms, airports, and industrial sites.

The art of training birds of prey originated in the Middle East and has spawned distinct cultural traditions across Asia, Europe, and North America. The technical term for a bird of prey is "raptor," a word derived from the Latin *rapere* (meaning "seize" or "capture"), which neatly evokes falconry's original practical purpose: to hunt. Raptors have wide, long tails that allow them to rapidly change trajectory mid-flight, and excellent vision—at least two or three times better than humans—that enables them to spot their prey from thousands of feet in the air. A diving peregrine falcon, for example, can attain speeds of up to 200 mph (320 kmh); their initial strike often kills prey on impact. The human hunting companion must trade other food for the prey before the bird destroys and devours it. In turn, the birds learn to trust that they'll be rewarded upon each successful capture, while falconers enjoy wild game with a few bite marks in it.

About 20 years ago, perceptive falconers picked up on a new ➤

108

through the air, the hook-beaked fowl present a terrifying aerial menace, but it's all a ruse: the falcons aren't actually hunting. They've been trained to fly in circles in exchange for food rewards. "For them, it's a game," explains Fortin, but it's not for the smaller birds. For prey, the threat is as real as it gets, so they stay away.

Like his cohorts, Fortin still takes his birds hunting, but it was conservation that originally drew him to the art of falconry. Having worked as a wildlife control specialist for nearly 30 years—he specialized in trapping beavers, coyotes, and foxes—he won a 2007 bid to perform wildlife management at Montreal–Dorval International Airport, Quebec, using falcons. Although Fortin had never actually practiced it before, he was down to learn.

Learning the techniques of falconry is a slow and careful process, one that's done mainly through apprenticeship and direct experience. Each falconer is part of a lineage of mentors who learned the art and passed it along. Despite a recent surge in popularity, the community of falconers remains comparatively small, in part because the practice is so demanding. Raptors aren't pets: they must hunt. Satisfying this need takes daily commitment and reliable access to good hunting territory. Fortin's training took almost four years and ② required him to travel to France several times.

Falconry isn't only labor intensive. Training and caring for these animals requires a special mentality, and it starts with knowing your place. "We can form a relationship, but it's one where the bird of prey is the king and we are their servants," Fortin explains. Raptors are extremely independent. "They don't need to be stroked like a cat or a dog," he says, "but they can quickly ➤

opportunity to exercise their symbiotic relationship with these birds that did not involve hunting: virtually harm-free wildlife management. In places like airports, where birds and other species pose a threat, deterrents such as sound cannons, flares, and audio recordings of predator noises are used to prevent animals from creating habitats. None of these deterrents are as consistently effective

as the fear of predatory birds seen and heard flying overhead.

While nuisance birds like seagulls eventually grow accustomed to deterrents, they will always flee a bird of prey. It's in their genes. Falconers exploit this evolutionary reflex without actually causing any unnecessary deaths (apart from to the farm-raised quail or day-old chicks they feed their raptors). Spiraling

03

01 Marc-André Fortin releases a falcon to chase geese off a farmer's field.

02 A falcon wears a helmet to help it remain calm during preparations for a chase.

03 Fortin observes a falcon that has just taken flight.

04 Jonathan Charlebois practices holding a falcon at Fortin's home.

04

05 An eagle perches on Fortin's outstretched arm.

06 Fortin swings a fake bird to call back his falcon. The falcon knows the command and will fly directly to the "toy" to end its chase.

07 The falcon returns from the chase. To celebrate, Fortin gives him a meaty snack.

08 Before any chase, Fortin makes sure that the GPS tags on the birds' legs are working.

(06)

(07)

(08)

learn to trust a human that provides reliable nourishment and opportunities to hunt." Within just a few weeks of such contact, a completely wild bird will form a strong rapport with a dedicated falconer.

Fortin has continued to pass his knowledge along to his employees, some of whom have advanced enough to train others. His company, Groupe Prévost-Fortin, has become a community of learning where all team members help each other improve their techniques. Fortin's employees often travel to participate in "field meets" with other falconers around North America. "Sometimes they're better than me," Fortin acknowledges.

He's preparing to retire and he's happy to know the art of falconry has grown thanks to his efforts. When the time comes to leave the commercial work behind, he'll go on serving these majestic predator birds and taking them into the wild to hunt, the way falconers have always done.

RAISING HONEY-BEES

The traditions of beekeeping are changing as falling bee populations threaten our food supply and the well-being of the planet. While regulators figure out how to protect honeybees from extinction, beekeepers are evolving their practices for a new era.

Bees are vital to the health of the Earth. Without their inadvertent labor of pollination—a byproduct of collecting nectar—about a third of the world's crops would never be fertilized. That's one of every three ➤

01

115

mouthfuls of food we eat. Despite their incredible gift to the planetary biome, bees aren't faring well in this era of human-first domination. Their populations are plummeting as a result of the usual catalytic suspects: extreme weather due to climate change, like droughts, wildfires, and floods; widespread use of pesticides in industrial agriculture and suburban backyards alike; habitat loss from urban sprawl and development; and tiny blood-sucking pests like the Varroa mite. We're waking up to the realities of our dependence on *Apoidea,* as well as to the charms of looking after it. As our species struggles to restore balance to our coexistence with nature at large, beekeeping is growing increasingly popular as a way of taking stewardship into one's own hands. We highlight the people behind the new rise of the honeybee.

CITY BEES

While pesticide use has made much of the countryside downright hostile to honeybees, the city has become an unlikely refuge for the busy little pollinators. With the combination of municipal anti-pesticide laws, abundant green spaces, and plenty of open rooftops, cities offer a uniquely welcoming habitat for bees, especially now that urban beekeeping is exploding in popularity among students, hobbyists, and entrepreneurs alike. Few cities are as bee-loving as Paris, home to more than 1,000 hives. Everyone is getting in on the action: a school for budding apiarists at the Luxembourg Gardens graduates more than 200 new beekeepers every year, and corporations schools, museums, and restaurants have also begun paying apiarists to keep bees on their rooftops, such as the École Militaire, Mandarin Oriental Hotel, and Opera Garnier. Community groups can ask for hives from the mayor's office, but demand has become so great that the city has been forced to put many of them on a waiting list, lest the number of bees outstrips the available pollen from parks, gardens, and cemeteries.

SOCIAL BEES

The growth in interest in beekeeping in recent years has also generated new kinds of social enterprises, such ➤ as Alvéole in Canada. Founded in Montreal in 2012, the urban beekeeping company offers customers the chance to host a hive on their rooftop or backyard, and to reap the sweet, golden reward. Wannabe beekeepers shouldn't let inexperience hold them back: Alvéole offers advice and assistance through classes, mentorship, and an accompanying app. The unique startup has even taken its honeybee innovation a step beyond and created a new model of raising bees—what co-founder Alex McLean calls "social beekeeping." Alvéole teamed up with l'Accueil Bonneau, a Montreal non-profit that helps homeless people reintegrate into society. Participants learn to tend the hives—all the way from caring for the bees to bottling and marketing the honey they help produce. The practice of raising bees fosters a feeling of connection with the natural world, and also a sense of investment in the well-being of the planet, not to mention oneself. Some describe the experience of beekeeping as a form of therapy, and many go on to become dedicated beekeepers year after year.

TRAVELING BEES

Once a stable profession for solitary types, beekeeping has lately transformed into a career for itinerant wanderers. Declining bee populations have created massive demand in the agriculture industry for well-kept hives to pollinate crops, meaning beekeepers have to travel. In this new world, bees are like livestock, except it isn't their honey that farmers want—it's their labor. Much of America's domesticated honeybee population now roams from town to town and state to state, pollinating various in-season crops along the way. One of the most important of these stops is California, where the majority of the world's almond supply is cultivated. The almond industry is growing so ➤

02 Madison Weir, a beekeeper with Alvéole, checks hives on the roof of RBC WaterPark Place in Toronto.

03 Beekeeper Sibyle Moulin performs maintenance on hives atop the roof of Notre-Dame Basilica in Paris.

02

04 Workers must climb up into the trees to reach all the pear blossoms that need pollinating in Hanyuan county, Sichuan province, China.

05 Since pesticide use destroyed local bee populations, pear blossoms have to be individually hand-pollinated.

fast even the beekeepers can't keep up—and with bee populations in rapid decline, almond companies are bracing for the worst: a world without bees. Everything is on the table, from genetically modified trees that self-pollinate to robot bees, but it's hard to beat the efficiency of the real thing. For the time being, migrating beekeepers, such as Colorado-based Lyle Johnston of Johnston Honey Farms, continue hauling their bees to wherever the food grows and the flowers bloom.

HUMAN BEES

In a part of China's Sichuan province known for its many pear orchards, heavy pesticide use has decimated the local bee population, so resident humans have replaced honeybees as the primary pollinators for the fruit trees. Using chicken feathers attached to sticks, farmworkers in Hanyuan County climb into the branches to fertilize female pear blossoms by hand, using pollen from little pots ➤

06 Will Nissen owns Five Star Honey Farms in Minot, North Dakota. Here, his bees have been transported to California to pollinate local almond trees.

07 A beekeeper from l'Accueil Bonneau examines a sheet of honeycomb at Montreal–Dorval International Airport.

hung around their necks. In this poor, rural region, hand pollination actually costs less than renting traveling colonies of honeybees. With bee populations plummeting around the world, it's worrisome to think that such intensive and cheap human labor could become the norm.

DANGER BEES

Honeybees perform their vital service all over the world, but not all honey is created equal. Himalayan giant honeybees in Nepal produce red-hued honey with psychotropic properties. Known as "mad honey," it sells on black markets in Asia for as much as $80 (€70) a pound. Made from the flowers of rhododendron trees in springtime, this hallucinogenic honey contains chemicals called *grayanotoxins,* which produce unappealing symptoms such as stomach pain and vomiting, but also offer relief for

08 A traditional honey hunter hangs in the air as he seeks to collect sheets of honeycomb that cling to cliff faces in Nepal.

09 "Mad honey" is so valuable that Kulung honey hunters put themselves at great personal risk to collect it.

10 A honey hunter climbs back up with his prize— still buzzing with giant Himalayan honeybees.

arthritis (and in larger doses, an unpleasant intoxication). It's so valuable that traditional honey hunters among the Kulung people risk their lives climbing tall cliffs to carve off large sections of hives for harvest. Before embarking on this death-defying honey hunt, they seek the help of Rangkemi, the guardian spirit of bees and monkeys, to bless and protect them. But the young in Kulung communities are losing their appetite for mad honey; most no longer wish to stay and risk their lives for the harvest. They have smartphones—they've tasted the fruits of modernity and found them just as sweet.

THIS CYCLE, THIS SEASON, THIS PLACE, THIS MOMENT, THESE FLOWERS

NEW YORK, USA

At Saipua's rural headquarters, *Sarah Ryhanen* helps people slow down, connect with others, and smell the flowers.

Sarah Ryhanen's suburban upbringing in Peekskill, New York, in the 1980s didn't exactly foretell the route she would later travel in life. Years before she founded Saipua, her floristry and soap-making brand, Ryhanen was no child of nature. "A lot of people assume that I grew up on a farm, but I really didn't. I grew up interested in getting my driver's license and collecting Absolute ads." Her frankness is refreshing.

Much has been written about Ryhanen and Saipua in the past decade. She's been characterized as a florist who "inspired an entirely new generation of floral designers" and an entrepreneur who uprooted her urban life to settle on a farm upstate. It'd be easy to imagine that Ryhanen was somehow following a clearly drawn out path. Instead, she gives the impression of a woman whose purpose is still very much burgeoning.

Ryhanen's love affair with flowers began around 2006, when she returned home from college, and, along with her partner, offered to help her mother launch the soap brand that would eventually become Saipua (the name means "soap" in Finnish). The newly discovered passion was a type of magic difficult to describe: "you've never really thought about flowers and all of a sudden they bring you so much joy." Ryhanen incorporated flower arranging into Saipua and set up shop in Brooklyn's Red Hook neighborhood. The boutique became an aesthete's Eden, and the neophyte's ➤

01 One of Ryhanen's floral arrangements.

02 Ryhanen's boutique quickly became an aesthetic Eden.

03 Ryhanen purchased a farm so that she could grow her own spectacular flowers.

charmingly wild and opulent arrangements quickly rose to prominence, adorning weddings, runways, and upscale events worldwide.

In 2011 Ryhanen purchased a 107-acre farm and called it World's End (a nod to the T.C. Boyle novel). At the time, the free-thinking entrepreneur was set on expanding her business by growing her own spectacular flowers. But as she settled into the realities of agricultural life, a new vision emerged for Saipua. Ryhanen began to notice that the simplest acts of living, things like cooking, decorating, or even weeding, were also opportunities to care for oneself and foster connections with others.

"What I'm after, essentially, is showing people—and learning at the same time—how to create a meaningful life. I say that out loud and it sounds a little bit ... funny. But I guess that's what I'm after, learning how to live."

Both statement and question, "how to live" guides Ryhanen and her team's journey toward a renewed way of being with each other and with nature. In the past year, Saipua has steered away from event work in order to focus more on educational programming. It ➤➤

SARAH RYHANEN

SARAH RYHANEN

04

04 The simple beauty of World's End.

05 Saipua has over 50 varieties of flowers.

06 Ryhanen strives to reconnect people with the bounty of the Earth.

05

06

SARAH RYHANEN

07 Saipua's educational programs encourage people to slow down and reflect.

08 Ryhanen hopes to inspire people to pay closer attention to the simple and lovely moments present in everyday life.

09 The farm's resident Icelandic sheep graze, manage pests, and fertilize flowers.

07

offers courses that span from tomato canning to soap making (a workshop given by Ryhanen's mom, Susan). In 2019 Ryhanen made the decision to run World's End with the help of women only.

A think tank for community living, Saipua conjures fresh perspectives "balancing the extraordinary and the whimsical with a sense of practicality and duty." This duty is part of a broader conversation about what we, as humans, value. "What we're doing," states Ryhanen, "is very political in some sense. This is the work of my life—I want to create something on the periphery of our capitalist cultural norms that can start to affect a few people and make space for something new to emerge."

It's difficult to predict exactly what Saipua and World's End will grow into once fully bloomed. For now, Ryhanen and her team find pleasure in encouraging self-replenishing life cycles. Because of a tight rotational grazing plan, for example, World's End's 20 Icelandic sheep consistently graze fresh grass, which keeps them healthy, and, in return, they fertilize the soil of Saipua's 50-plus varieties of ravishing flowers.

The all-female World's End crew also welcomes visitors. Whether for an afternoon or a full-week residency, Saipua's rural headquarters are designed to provide a place for people to slow down, engage in meaningful conversation, and indulge in what Ryhanen calls "the art of noticing": "A very simple thing that I can teach people is the cycle of nature as it relates to flowers and plants. Trees blossom in the spring and make fruit in the fall. That is the cycle. My hope is that the next time people notice flowering trees they're able to place themselves in this cycle, in the moment, the season, a little better. That's something very powerful that happens here at World's End; people come and experience all kinds of different flowers and plants, and they are taking that with them wherever they live."

DATE SELLERS

For centuries, Bedouin nomads were fueled by the calories of dates as they traveled back and forth across the Arabian Peninsula. Today, the sugary fruit is the star of the Unaizah Date Festival.

Most storylines about Saudi Arabia center around the kingdom's deep social conservatism, vast oil wealth, or geopolitical machinations in the greater Middle East. In looking to understand a country attempting to modernize its economy and re-engineer its society all while retaining traditional power structures, the Unaizah date market helps bring things into focus. Since 1980, the date festival has been steadily growing into its present form, a 70-day auction in late summer that generates as much as $300 (€275) million through the sale of thousands of tons of dates. ➤

It's hard to travel around Middle Eastern and North African countries for long without consuming dates: lush pods of sugar and fiber wrapped around a slender (and easily avoided) seed. They come in blacks and yellows and reds and browns, enjoyed fresh or packed together until the huddled mass of fruit starts to caramelize into a single molten mass.

Dates have long been a part of the land that now forms the Kingdom of Saudi Arabia. A millennium and some centuries ago, the prophet Muhammad exhorted Muslims in the month of Ramadan to "break your fast with a date, for it is purifying."

Today, a date palm sits at the heart of the official emblem of Saudi Arabia, with two crossed swords guarding the symbol for the kingdom's heritage.

The market that hosts the Unaizah festival is enormous: a giant plaza as wide as a football field and twice as long. Things get moving early, before the desert sun turns the concrete surface into a hotplate.

"We'll stop by at midnight to check that all of the dates are fine," explains Ali Muhammad al-Khuwaiter, a date merchant from Unaizah re-selling a few surplus date boxes from the wholesale lots under the market's titanic sunshades. "Right after the dawn prayer, everybody starts to appear, and it all wraps up at about 9 a.m."

From the ground level, it's hard to see past the hundreds of Saudis in white robes (plus a few other Gulf citizens) milling about the business end of the date cart trains, where jolly and less-than-jolly auctioneers call out the ever-escalating prices per box.

The crowd is overwhelmingly male, save for a few women who appear to be quietly scouting out starting prices and date quality for upcoming auction lots. Indian and Pakistani porters brush by, maneuvering clutches of date-filled carts to the loading docks in the back, while a few ne'er-do-wells (a rough translation for the colloquial term *derbawi*), carry out minor acts of teen rebellion by wearing non-white robes and pestering us for Snapchat selfies.

Under all the chaos, though, lies market machinery of ruthless efficiency. Trains of metal carts stretch far into the distance, held in perfectly straight lines by slender grooves cast into the concrete. Each night, dates are loaded up on the 15 trains, ordered from highest to lowest quality, ready to be rapid-fire auctioned off, detached from the train, and taken to waiting cars or trucks, or even motorbikes.

The entire market lies on a slight downward slope, meaning the carts—engineered to ease up on their internal brakes as more weight is placed on their shelves—roll forward nearly of their own accord from the sellers' drop-off point to the buyers' collection stalls.

"We applied physics in order to sell dates!" exclaims festival director Yusuf al-Dukhayel back at the command center, noting that the new set-up needs just 35 full-time workers compared to the old market's 120. He first saw the carts at a famers ➤

03

04

market in the Netherlands, where he owns a date-exporting business, and then set about convincing the Unaizah Municipal Council, along with the Unaizah Chamber of Commerce, to invest in its own gravity-cart system. "The 2030 [Saudi] Vision talks about reducing production costs and encouraging innovation. If you can come up with a new idea, it's better than any amount of petroleum," he says.

Most striking about all of this feverish economic activity is that it seems driven not by some top-down expert plan, but by Unaizans' fierce dedication to putting their city on the map. The town's independent streak

stems from a long-standing, if subdued, resistance to the kingdom's efforts to impose a uniform sense of "Saudi-ness."

"By God, we will protect our lands or die trying" was the message sent by Unaizans to future Saudi king Abdulaziz al-Saud in 1904, offering help in his efforts to unify the kingdom but pledging a fierce fight if not left in some degree of peace. As a result, the Al-Sulaim dynasty still governs Unaizah by written treaty, rather than a member of the vast Al Saud family.

Saudi Vision 2030 may provide some official cover for Unaizah's latest

efforts to develop a local economy based around a local identity, given the shout-out in the plan to the "cultural richness and diversity" of Saudi Arabian society.

True, there is hardly any more formal democracy in Unaizah than in Riyadh, while date production is likely dwarfed by government subsidies financed by oil income. In trying to secure Unaizah's reputation, the joint work of local rulers, merchants, and farmers has helped ensure that in one place, however briefly, everything works as it should.

The fruit of their efforts is reflected in the glint of the sun on a

05 Carts full of sold dates are hauled off to the rear of the market as the last few auctions wrap up.

06 The Unaizah Date Festival is best known for its *sukkari asfar*, or "yellow sugary" dates.

07 Auctioneers take a cut of each lot sold, and can earn tens or even hundreds of thousands of riyals in a single season.

06

thousand date cart frames, echoed in the sound of a thousand date lot bids. As the day begins to heat up in the mid-morning sun, the last few date cart trains are auctioned off and rolled away. Already, attendants in tractors are hauling long chains of carts up to the top of the slope, re-racking the system for another day of dates.

07

CRÉPISSAGE

As militant attacks get closer, the Malian town of Djenné defiantly continues its annual tradition of replastering its ancient mud mosque.

The evening before the *crépissage*, the annual replastering of the Great Mosque of Djenné, Balphady Yaro is throwing a party for his friends and neighbors in the town's Konofia neighborhood.

Rickety plastic chairs and tables line the winding streets around Djenné's main square, where the mosque looms over the town's low mud-brick houses. There are plates of *riz au gras*—tasty rice with meat and vegetables—and chilled soft drinks. Ivorian *Coupé-Décalé* music reverberates on soft mud walls.

Djenné, a town of about 35,000 in the central region of Mali, is famous for its traditional mud-brick architecture and its UNESCO-protected mosque. Fifty-two feet (16 meters) high and built on a 300-foot-long (90-meter) platform to protect it from flooding, the mosque is the world's largest mud-brick ➤

139

01 A group of women carrying water needed for the mud mixture. Men and boys are responsible for bringing the mud to the mosque, while and women and girls are tasked with bringing water from the river.

The increasing instability in Mali's central region—fueled by inter-tribal conflicts and growing numbers of militant and jihadist groups exploiting the absence of state security forces—now threatens Djenné and its sacred annual ritual. Local militants—some linked to the Group for the Support of Islam and Muslims (JNIM), formed by the 2017 merger of several extremist groups operating in Mali—have invaded towns, destroyed markets, and spread their influence in central Mali.

So far, Djenné and its mosque have been spared, but the security situation in the region continues to deteriorate, and more frequent attacks are being carried out in Djenné's orbit.

building. Touching up its walls each year—called *crépissage,* the French word for "plastering"—is a proud and exuberant ritual that involves the whole town.

"The crépissage is the most important event of the year, even bigger than Eid al-Fitr, marking the end of Ramadan, or Tabaski [the Malian equivalent of Christmas]," says Yaro, a 30-year-old lawyer and host of the celebration, known as *la nuit de veille.*

Sitting under a tarpaulin strung between two neem trees, Yaro watches as the crowds sway through the street. The partygoers won't sleep until after the crépissage. The revelry will strengthen them ahead of tomorrow's big task, Yaro claims, sipping a soft drink. "Tonight we party, and tomorrow we will celebrate our mosque and Djenné's cultural heritage."

The residents of Djenné come together to put a new layer of clay on their mosque every April, just before the rainy season. The crépissage is both a necessary maintenance task to prevent the mosque's walls from crumbling and an elaborate festival that celebrates Djenné's heritage, faith, and community. It's also an act of defiance.

"We knew that the militants were getting closer to Djenné," says town chief Sidi Yéya Maiga at his home the day before the crépissage. This year the town council even took the extraordinary step of debating whether or not to cancel their cherished tradition.

In an act of collective resistance, they decided the show must go on.

On the day before the crépissage, Nouhoum Touré, the a master among Djenné's 250 masons, heads down to the riverbank to check on the mud that has been left to soak for 20 days.

02 Children walking through a pit of mud in front of the mosque.

03 The crépissage is the most important event in Mali.

03

It's the height of the dry season, and the river has shrunk to shallow puddles and inlets. The round pools that store clay until it's time for the crépissage look like pockmarks on the riverbed.

The mud comes from further down the river and is transported here by trucks and donkey carts. Younger masons then break the blocks into smaller chunks and mix them with water. In the final stages, rice husks are added to the mud, turning it into a soft and sticky paste. The rice works like a glue, holding the mud together and keeping it from cracking as it dries. The young masons then carry the mixture, in wicker baskets, to pits in front of the mosque in preparation for the event.

Early in the morning on the long-awaited day of the crépissage, Djenné's residents gather by the mosque and wait for Touré to smear the first blob of mud on the wall. This is the starting gun.

There is a roar from the crowd as dozens of young men—some masons, some apprentices—run to the mosque. Smaller groups of boys raise wooden ladders against the mosque wall.

Carrying wicker baskets full of dripping-wet clay from the pits next to the mosque, the young men begin scrambling up the façade, using ladders to reach the wooden poles protruding from the walls. Perching perilously on the wooden scaffolding, they pick up large blobs of clay and smear them on the walls.

Nientao, the mosque's guardian, weaves through the crowd, his pockets filled with sweets for the workers. Thousands of muddy feet trample the paths around the mosque. As the sun begins to rise over Djenné, turning shapeless shadows into dark silhouettes, a group of boys and masons tackle the minarets from the roof of the mosque.

Four hours later, the morning sun shines on the newly plastered mosque. Dark, wet clay patches on the dried mud give it a sickly look.

Touré is covered in mud all the way from his plastic sandals, which have miraculously stayed on his feet, to the top of his turban. "I think we did very well," he says, sitting in the shade of the mosque. "Normally, we ➤

04 Young men and boys run down the front steps of the mosque after dropping off baskets of mud.

05 Nouhoum Touré, Djenné's grand mason, taking a break inside the mosque.

re-mud the mosque over two days. This time we managed to get it done in only one day."

A little later, there is a crack as the loudspeakers come on, then the sound of Djenné's mayor, Balfine Yaro, clearing his throat. Everyone looks on in silence as he makes his way to the front of the crowd. He declares Djenneka Raws the winning team. Djelika Kantao and Yoboucaïna have prevailed. For the winners, there is pride, honor, and a cash prize of 50,000 West African francs, or about $90 (€80).

"With the money," says Kantao, beaming with pride, "I will buy new solar panels for the neighborhood, so we no longer have to live in darkness."

07

06 The Djenné mosque the day before the crépissage.

07 Residents carrying mud, from pits to the mosque ahead of the crépissage.

08 Men on handmade ladders plastering the mosque.

143

FOREST GUARDIANS

The traditional way of life of the Ogiek people is under threat from the rapacious Kenyan government and the encroachment of industry. But the Indigenous group is fighting back, using the tools of modern technology to draw supporters to their cause.

In an area considered to be one of the cradles of humankind, the last hunter-gatherers in East Africa have learned to enshrine environmental activism in their way of life. The Ogiek are an Indigenous group whose traditions and practices are **01** deeply entwined with the natural ➤

147

world and reflect a perfect symbiosis with their forest home: gathering wild fruits and roots, selectively hunting species that aren't endangered, and keeping bees high in the trees. About 20,000 Ogiek still live in a 222,000-acre area of Kenya's Mau and Mount Elgon forests that is swiftly being chewed up by the hungry jaws of development.

For decades, the Ogiek's sustainable lifestyle has been under assault. The Kenyan government has repeatedly sought to expel them from their traditional territory—appropriating and re-allocating their land to forestry and agriculture companies—under the cruelly ironic pretext that the Ogiek are harming the environment. In fact, the opposite is true: the Ogiek consider themselves guardians of the forests, a responsibility that lies at the core of their identity; even the term *Ogiek* means "caretaker of all plants and wild animals.'" Sadly, the Ogiek are no strangers to having to fight for their ancestral homeland. Prior to their current battle with the Kenyan government over their rights to the Mau, Forest, they were enduring the advancements of British colonialists as far back as the 1920s. Despite a long history of resisting oppression, the accelerated pace of natural destruction now poses a seemingly insurmountable threat. Between 1973 and 2009, 30 percent of the Mau Forest was cut down, and in the last 15 years alone, 100,000 acres have been destroyed. Clear-cutting and burning convert old-growth forests to barren landscapes, where mudslides pose an increasing threat. The Ogiek are terrified that in the end they will be completely dominated and marginalized by invading settlers. They view land appropriations as a surefire death warrant for the forest, and by extension, their identity. When the forests are mowed

01 Clare Rono walks toward the Mau Forest Complex to collect water.

02 The Ogiek have been practicing beekeeping in these trees for centuries.

03 Ogiek elders say that "there are now less trees—and less bees."

04 Ogiek community member Jackson Warionga.

(04)

down to make way for farms and development, it's a direct attack on the cultural birthright of Ogiek children.

If the forests disappear, crucial habitats are destroyed, which in turn erodes traditional Ogiek practices like hunting. The most important game for Ogiek hunters is the tree hyrax, a small, rotund mammal that grazes on leaves and grasses, and that is, surprisingly, most closely related to the elephant, though the largest ones are only two feet (0.6 meters) long. With the shrinking forests, the Ogiek are already hunting less and less, and despite their resistance to encroaching development, they've begun to adopt the lifestyle of farming.

The Ogiek tradition of beekeeping has proven more resilient. They keep hives in hollow cedar logs hung high up in tall trees. The honey is produced by small black African honeybees from the flowers of the *Dombeya goetzeni* plant, which gives it a distinctive flavor. Ogiek men collect the honey by climbing vines and burning dry moss to smoke the hives. To better sustain the tradition in these times of danger and upheaval, Ogiek women now keep hives as well, on the ground rather than in the trees.

Some forms of modernization are more positive. Many Ogiek now carry smartphones, which they primarily use to preserve their traditions, advocate for themselves online, and advertise their situation to sympathetic audiences abroad. Search the Ogiek on Instagram ➤

FOREST GUARDIANS

05 Ogiek community members from Molo village, Mau Forest.

06 Lifestyles change with the landscape. The Ogiek now grow crops such as corn.

07 Ogiek beekeeper William Kalegu on his way to inspect the beehives.

08 Ogiek elders wearing traditional hunting clothing made of hyrax skin.

05

06

and you'll find many posts related to their struggle (and of course to their honey).

It's thanks to this commitment to self-advocacy that they were able to convince Minority Rights Group International to bring Brussels-based photographer Dia Takacsova to Kenya to document the culture and traditions of the Ogiek in 2018, just over a year after the African Court on Human and Peoples' Rights ruled that the Kenyan government was violating the rights of the Ogiek people by evicting them from their land. The court stated that the Ogiek deserve compensation, but the Kenyan government has so far failed to act meaningfully on the ruling. Despite the decision, the Ogiek have been subjected to continued harassment, intimidation, and more land appropriation.

The Ogiek want the Kenyan government to stop allocating the rights of this ancient forest to logging companies, farmers, and wildlife parks, and to enact an Ogiek Land Act that would give the Indigenous people the right to inhabit and conserve the Mau Forest. The Ogiek have formed several grassroots organizations to fight for their heritage, such as the Ogiek Welfare Council and ECOTERRA Kenya. While they want nothing more than to maintain their ancient connection to the forest, the Ogiek aren't afraid to build new connections online to achieve their aims.

07

08

GREENHOUSE GROWERS

Climate change is threatening the viability of millions of small farms in India, but an innovative new greenhouse solution is transforming the lives of vulnerable farmers.

For small-scale farmers in dry regions of India, water supply can too easily mean the difference between life and death. The long droughts, extended heat waves, and unpredictable rainfall brought about by global warming have proven disastrous for many of India's 146 million small farms, 85 percent of which now lose more money than they make. ➤

01 Yadav Bhavanth's nieces and nephew get ready to take produce to the local market.

02 Bhavanth and his wife, Bujji, grow tomatoes in their greenhouse, located on the family farm near Laxmapur village in Telangana state. Bhavanth was the first to purchase a greenhouse from Kheyti.

01

02

During a recent three-year drought, more than 11,000 smallholder farmers committed suicide, mostly in response to crop failure and unpaid loans. Things are only getting worse as the climate crisis deepens; by 2030, India's water demand is expected to be double its supply.

A new kind of greenhouse is making a dramatic difference for some vulnerable farmers. Hyderabad-based non-profit Kheyti has created an affordable and effective greenhouse system that helps small farms bring stability to their crop production and withstand the worst effects of climate change. The company is calling it the "smart farmer revolution."

Unlike typical glass greenhouses, Kheyti's modular Greenhouse-in-a-Box (GIB) is designed to keep light and heat out. Draped across a simple metal frame, the system uses four layers of breathable aluminum-coated netting to stop pests, partially reflect sunlight (preventing crop damage from excessive heat), and reduce water loss through evaporation. The technology allows impoverished farmers to use 90 percent less water, grow seven times more food, and achieve better and more dependable yields, thereby helping to stabilize income. Kheyti's system costs about half the price of other greenhouses, and the company says that after six years farmers can expect to earn $100 (€90) a month, the equivalent of one year's revenue under normal conditions.

Kheyti's greenhouse also employs micro-irrigation, or drip irrigation, a technology that was first commercialized over 80 years ago but has not reached the vast majority of farmers in India until now. Drip irrigation confers much better water efficiency than the reliance on seasonal rainfall. Coupled with its heat-resistant netting, the Kheyti greenhouse requires just 265 gallons (1,000 liters)

05

06

07

03 Venkatesh Appala grows bell peppers in in his Kheyti greenhouse, and is using the extra income to save for his daughter's dowry.

04 Goats eat tomatoes in an empty farming field in a rural area near Laxmapur village, just north of Hyderabad city.

05 Katikala Shyamala, 43, the village sarpanch or headwoman, is pictured in her office in Laxmapur village. She was the first woman to sign up for a greenhouse.

06 Capsicum (bell peppers) grow in the greenhouse owned by Venkatesh Appala, 45, near Laxmapur village in Telangana state.

07 Bujji Bhavanth, 32, works in her small shop run out of her home in Laxmapur, Thanda.

per day, which is 20 percent of what farmers would otherwise use in an open farming plan, according to co-founder Shradha Sharma.

Launched in 2015, Kheyti—Sanskrit for "farming"—offers more than just specialized technology. To help achieve the best results, the social enterprise conducts in-the-field training workshops and provides advice via mobile devices (80 percent of India's farmers own some sort of smartphone). Kheyti even built in a supply chain. The GIB package comes bundled with added seeds and fertilizer, and Kheyti is also set up to connect farmers with produce retailers.

Since most of India's farmers don't have the capital to purchase a greenhouse, Kheyti has partnered with the country's Bank of Baroda to help farmers obtain flexible loans. After an initial down payment of 30,000 rupees, or about $471 (€423), farmers

can pay back their loan in installments after each growing season.

One of the best parts of Kheyti's approach is the culture of sharing and collaboration it creates between participating farmers. When they sign up for a greenhouse, farmers automatically join a collective that meets weekly to compare notes and discuss best practices. Sometimes they pitch in and help with each other's crops. These extra supports, both from Kheyti and the collective, enable farmers like Katikala Shyamala, the head woman of a small village called Laxmapur, to operate a greenhouse while still managing other responsibilities and raising children.

Kheyti co-founder Sathya Raghu Mokkapati made it his mission to help India's poor farmers after witnessing a penniless farmer resort to eating mud. An accountant by training, Mokkapati understood ➤

08 Local farmers pose for a portrait outside of Kheyti's hub farms near Depalle village.

GREENHOUSE GROWERS

the importance of small farmers being able to access financing and the difference it could make for their profitability, but he knew he would need more hands-on experience to tackle the problem. After leaving his corporate job, he and Sharma spent three and a half years farming a hundred-acre plot and working with nearly 8,000 farmers to try different methods and crops.

Along with their third co-founder, Saumya (who doesn't use a surname), and some help from engineering students at Northwestern University and Stanford University, the entrepreneurs created a design that would mitigate the effects of extreme climate variability. Once finalized, Kheyti began performing proofs of concept with 150 farmers in 15 villages in 2018; the trials proved immediately and immensely successful. Early participants found they were able to produce the same yield in their small greenhouses as an entire acre outside, and use the leftover profits to send their children to school.

In the past year, Kheyti has worked to bring on another 1,000 farmers—all low-income women farmers—in collaboration with the Society for Elimination of Rural Poverty. Kheyti's ambitions go much further: they aim to reach 100,000 farmer families by 2025. If all goes well, their greenhouse tech has the potential to expand internationally. Smallholder farmers make up one of the world's largest constituencies of impoverished people, and yet these farms are responsible for growing 80 percent of the food on the planet. Around the world, there are half a billion small farms struggling to survive due to factors like poor yields, environmental volatility, and market fluctuations. If it scales, Kheyti's simple, innovative greenhouse solution could have a transformative impact on the lives of millions.

OF WINERIES AND WILD-FIRES: GRAPES OF WRATH

Winemakers *Lore and Skyla Olds* are implementing vigilant new growing practices to safeguard against the ravages of unchecked climate change.

In the fall of 2017, Lore and Skyla Olds, the father-and-daughter team behind Sky Vineyards, were sitting inside their family home on the eastern-facing side of Mount Veeder—a summit on the Mayacamas mountain range that separates Napa Valley and Sonoma in Northern California. The Oldses had spent that afternoon crushing grapes on the property of their winemaking neighbor and friend, Nic Coturri of Sonoma Mountain Winery.

After a long day of labor, Skyla and Lore invited Nic and extended family members over for a celebratory meal. Guests arrived for dinner, having passed through the property's front gate down a slope containing vines of Syrah en route to the Oldses' home. The fall had been unusually hot and dry, and that Sunday night temperatures stayed summerlike, with wind gusts reaching 45 mph (73 kmh). Skyla's niece, whose young eyes were alert to the elements, said the weather that night seemed "really dangerous."

A few hours later, the first of a series of wildfires in Northern California had started—they would burn 245,000 acres in the region. The Oldses saw a billowing column of blackish-gray smoke above Mount Veeder that would later consume the house where they had feasted together only days before. When all was said and done, flames had torn through 199 of Sky Vineyards' 200 acres.

Lore and Skyla were among dozens of vineyard owners in the Napa and Sonoma wine region to sustain significant damage to their property. As the Earth's temperature continues to rise and wildfires become an increasingly common threat, growers and viticulturists are being forced to adjust and adapt their practices to safeguard against similar disasters in the future.

Miraculously, nearly 11 months later, on a clear afternoon in late August, Skyla, Lore, and Nic were all back to work at Sky Vineyards, preparing for an unlikely harvest. The Oldses' property is still surrounded by colonies of Knobcone pines charred black from the fires; >>

160

02

03

04

05

162

01 Skyla Olds inspects harvest-ready grapes on her family's vineyard one year after the 2017 wildfires.

02 Nic Coturri, neighbor and friend to the Oldses, samples his wine from Sonoma Mountain Winery.

03 Skyla shows off a fresh bottle of Coturri's all-natural wine.

04 Because the wildfires mostly burned dry brush, Sky Vineyards' vines survived the fires, and produced grapes the next year.

05 A vine-side picnic lunch before the harvest.

06 In 2017, wildfire raced across 199 of Sky Vineyards' 200 acres.

06

they stand out against the newly regenerating earth like skinny black ghosts. Skyla and her father have been living in trailers. At 72, Lore is vigorous and jolly. He first learned to make wine in 1971, while working at HillCrest Vineyard in Oregon. In 1973, Lore's parents helped him and Skyla's mother purchase the land on which they built their home and planted their vineyard.

As remote as this property may appear to be, a creek that runs through its center has drawn people for millennia. The Wappo people once lived here—the word *Napa* comes from their language, and means "land of plenty"—and the foundation of an old homestead structure also remains on site.

It was that resource—water—that was incalculably valuable when the fires arrived in 2017. The one acre of property that didn't burn held the vineyard's winery: a large classic barn on the edge of the creek that was built by Lore's father using reclaimed wood from Pier 69 in San Francisco. The only sign of fire: a bit of black soot near the top, where, Skyla says, flames just kissed the building. The creek acted like a protective moat around the barn, safeguarding the Oldses' entire stock of barrelled, bottled, and fermenting wines.

"We have been feeling the effects of climate change for the last few years," says Skyla, standing at a large table inside the barn and affixing labels to bottles of their rosé. "We always started picking grapes in the middle of September in the 40 years we've been up here." In the last three years, she says, they've started picking in the middle of August—dramatically earlier than ever before. Global warming is showing itself through the dates of their harvests.

After decades of working and adapting his farming techniques to the land and climate, Lore landed on a wine-making method that starts the fermentation process using commercial yeast and then adds small amounts of sulfites to the wine after it is bottled. Otherwise, the Oldses' wine is organic and made from sustainable techniques—including their decision to not till the soil.

Yet it was that untilled soil, and the dry grass at the base of the vines, that meant the vineyard had no protective firewall. Luckily, the fires began post-harvest, so the grapes escaped the infamous "smoke taint" that many wines have acquired in the recent years of pre-harvest wildfires. A charred flavor seeps into the grapes and, according to Skyla, though the resulting wine can pass as interesting, more often than not, this burnt note ruins the wine completely. Lore and Skyla have so far avoided this fate, but they can't rely on similar luck in the future.

But given the growing threat of wildfire due to climate change, what can they do to prevent this kind of loss in the future? Property owners are supposed to clear 100 feet (30 meters) of brush around structures; this significantly curtails fire from spreading when it starts. "Lore spends so much time cutting brush," says Skyla. "He wants to take a whole year off wine making just to clear brush."

Controlled burns are one of the most effective practices for preventing wildfires on similarly disastrous scales. Unfortunately, it's hard to get the public to support them, or the resources to conduct them successfully. In the meantime, annual droughts and overgrown forests create an unchecked natural tinderbox of dead material.

"There's preventable fire and non-preventable fire," says Skyla. "I'm worried there's going to be more of the latter—but I also think everyone's going to be more attentive to keeping their 100 feet of clearance, and more attentive to conditions because of the experience we just had." After all, the Oldses can't count on the barn being miraculously saved after every fire.

Skyla described the experience of first finding it untouched. Before the fires, the grapes hadn't yet

LORE AND SKYLA OLDS

07 Skyla's father, Lore Olds, established Sky Vineyard in 1973.

08 Lore's father built the winery barn using reclaimed wood from Pier 69 in San Francisco. A specter of the flames is visible along the roofline.

09 Charred remnants from the fire are visible throughout the vineyard.

09

10 The vintage grape press used by Lore and Skyla for nearly all of their grapes.

11 A sweeping view of Sky Vineyards' pre-harvest grapes surrounded by charred knobcone pines.

12 The front gate at Sky Vineyards also survived the fire.

10

11

12

166

started to ferment, but when she walked inside the barn for the first time, she could hear the process at work, as the yeast ate away at the sugars and released carbon dioxide. "To have this hope that there was still something to come back to was incredible," she says.

At the picnic table, next to resilient fields of Syrah and Zinfandel, we sit and drink the Riesling Skyla and Lore had made for the first time from grapes purchased from a nearby vineyard. Skyla tells us how, one day, she'd like to grow green grapes of her own, and Lore discusses how, for him, wine making is an unending intellectual pursuit. Even before the week's harvest begins, the Oldses' comeback is well under way.

> To have this hope that there was still something to come back to was incredible.

TAKING ROOT: URBAN FARMERS EXPERIMENT WITH GROWING EXOTIC PLANTS

Agri-food technologist *Hamidou Abdoulaye Maïga* left his native Niger to come to Canada. Now he's bringing beloved African plants to his adopted home.

A blazing sun hits USC Canada's cropland in Montreal's West Island. "It's a great year for ethnic vegetables," says Hamidou Abdoulaye Maïga as he surveys a 2,000-square-foot (185-square-meter) patch of land on loan from the organization, whose mission consists of preserving seed diversity.

He points to some of the veggies in the ground. "We have okra *m'hrani*—and that's *kiwano*. When ripe, it's very juicy. We used to plant it in Kenya by the roadside on the way to the fields. It was a long way, and we'd get thirsty," he explains, while he bites into a small, tender white-but-almost-green fruit that looks like a shelled pea: a fresh peanut. "Apparently it's my specialty!" laughs the Montrealer by adoption.

While for some these crops may be new, for others they are as familiar as peppers, basil, and cucumbers—which is exactly why Maïga has been focused on them for nearly 10 years. When he moved from his native Niger in 2008, the accounting graduate quickly swapped rows of numbers for rows of soil. He started with a three-year program at Saint-Hyacinthe's Institut de Technologie Agroalimentaire, then created his own company so he ➤

168

01 USC Canada's urban farm in Montreal, populated with ancient, exotic, and native plants.

02 Hamidou Abdoulaye Maïga picking fresh peanuts.

03 Freshly picked African eggplant.

could grow organic herbs, ornamental plants, and exotic ancient, and native vegetables in Montreal. At first, without a greenhouse or extensive tracts of land, his plants took over the basement of the housing co-op where he lived with his family. Now, a few years later, Hamidou Horticulture products can be found all over the island—most predominantly in the Grand Potager greenhouse in Verdun and the USC Canada cropland in Senneville.

Maïga's passion for agriculture was sown a long time ago. Parallel to his career as an accountant, Maïga worked on his family's farm in Niger, where he was in charge of delivering fruits and vegetables. "We were making organic baskets without even knowing such a thing existed." While he nurtured the dream of living on his native land, the lack of access to training and resources was a harsh reality he couldn't ignore. So he ended up

in Quebec, determined to create a network. In his opinion, a partnership is the key to accessibility, which remains one of the biggest challenges in urban areas. "At first, I carried my burden alone. I mentioned what I was doing to people I met here and

there, and they would say: 'Yes, we'll help you.' And they showed up." Then, so did success, which wasn't too far behind for Maïga and his modest team of volunteers.

The growing interest in urban agriculture may have something to ➤

It was important to me that my girls kept in touch with their African roots.

04

do with it. It's usually by ordering horticultural advice from organizations in exchange for parcels of land that Maïga circumvents the issue of access to territory. But the challenges of stability and market access remain.

"Our clientele is there, but they don't know we exist. If we could work with five or six restaurants, the same number of grocery stores, and maybe a point of sale, it would already be a good start." With that in mind, Maïga's business is quite well positioned to take off this year, thanks to the recent involvement of Montreal-based Arrivage, a supply network for restaurant professionals that has cut out costly agents.

Maïga says that he's now "managed to partner with restaurant owners, who buy my products directly." These include the owner of the Le Virunga restaurant, proud sponsor of African eggplant seeds. "The idea is to tackle one small project at a time. From the seeds we sow in people's minds, many more collaborations will arise."

A FERTILE FUTURE

While urban agriculture already requires ingenuity, farming exotic foods in Quebec sounds like a real feat. And yet: "Species like the peanut and *bissap* [hibiscus] can easily grow here. It's just a matter of choosing early-maturing varieties that react well to brief periods of intense heat," explains Maïga, a strong advocate for biodiversity. "From year to year, we build up our seed bank—everything is stored and identified. When a plant performs well, we reuse its seeds the following year. The new plants react even better since they come from vegetables that have already adapted to their environment. That's how genetic adaptation works."

Accessibility, freshness, traceability, eco-responsibility, biodiversity—the list of benefits is long. Yet the motivation behind the project is something else entirely. "It was important to me that my girls kept in touch with their African roots. Now, we're beginning to see more fresh products in our grocery stores, but when we got here, it was more complicated," Maïga says.

Though there's still a lot of room for improvement in Montreal, imagine what it's like in the country. The entrepreneur believes that a lot of newcomers choose to settle in the big city for precisely that reason. "By providing better access to foreign products throughout the entire region, we could help decentralize the immigrant population." Maïga knows better than anyone that cultural bonds can yield something very strong. "You know, a man once grabbed my arm and told me, 'I never thought I'd ever see this vegetable again, do you realize?' That's why we do this work." And that's also why, as you read these lines, a baobab tree is slowly growing—in Saint-Hyacinthe.

04 Maïga points out an okra tree.

05 Maïga's work preserves biodiversity and provides newcomers to Montreal with a local source of fresh African produce.

SHEEP HERDERS

How beloved, centuries-old traditions of rounding up sheep in Europe bring communities together.

The age-old traditions that govern the lives of shepherds are as varied as they are widespread. They form the architecture of entire villages and regions. The customs and cultures are built into the land, woven through communities, and passed down to eager new generations. Though deeply rooted in the past, these ways of life illuminate a promising view for the future.

RÉTTIR, ICELAND

Come mid-September in Iceland, the crowds of tourists have decreased; the long, sun-filled days of summer have turned a bit darker; and a chill in the air has compelled locals to dust off thick wool sweaters. An event takes place this time of year that excites the entire island: the annual sheep roundup, or, as it's known by locals, *réttir*.

One of Iceland's oldest cultural traditions, réttir is a community celebration that draws people from ➤ **01**

01 A young Icelandic woman searches for her sheep at the annual sheep round-up. Each sheep is tagged on its ear with the farm it belongs to, though rumor has it some experienced farmers can recognize their sheep across the *rett* (the pen in which they are sorted) purely by sight.

02 A young shepherd guides her family's sheep back to their farm after sorting them at the *rett*. People of all ages take part in the annual sheep round-ups.

near and far. Joined by loyal sheep-dogs, tourists and locals of all ages set out on foot and horseback to gather sheep that have been roaming since early spring, fattening themselves on moss, wild berries, and pristine Icelandic grass.

The demanding endeavor of rounding up sheep can take as long as two weeks. Organized community teams donning neon vests, walkie-talkies, and simple noisemakers stay in mountain huts while searching. The long days are followed by nights of traditional meals, music, and drinking.

Sara Reykdal, 41, and her younger sister þórunn Eyjólfsdóttir, known as Tota, have been doing this for generations. Their family's farm, Starrastadir, which means "place of the blackbird," is located in the village of Sauðárkrókur on the northern coast of Iceland, known for its striking coastlines, black-sand beaches, and sweeping vistas. Starrastadir, which has been in the family for nearly 10 decades, is home to 400 ewes—a medium-sized farm by Icelandic standards.

Sara's 18-year-old son, Úlfar Hörður Sveinsson, with his calm and steady demeanor, doesn't seem to tire from long days in the saddle

03 Alma Snæland, 15, from Skagafjörður, Iceland, attended the sheep round-ups regularly while growing up. She doesn't participate in them much anymore, but still likes to watch and be part of the festivities, as they remind her of her childhood.

04 Locals sort the sheep in a ring-shaped *rett*. Sara Reykdal and her son, Úlfar, take inventory of the sheep they have rounded up for the winter at their farm, Starrastadir, located in northern Iceland.

03

searching for sheep: this is merely one part of the hard work. Sorting the sheep in a traditional live-stock ring called a *rett* is another.

He enthusiastically joins in, along with his mother, aunt, and the rest of their team.

The sorting process returns sheep to the farms they came from many months earlier. Packed tightly in a ring made of stone, wood, or metal, the sheep trot and buck wildly as people of all ages try their hand at wrangling them into the proper enclosure. A tag on each sheep's ear tells sorters which one belongs where, although many long-time farmers claim to recognize faces from across the ring.

A cacophony of bleating, children's laughter, and Icelandic chatter fills the air as wool sweaters, shed from all the hard work, pile up on side fences. The energy is at once playful and focused. After the central ring is empty and the sheep sorted, people ➤

04

05

05 The whole town participates in the *réttir,* or roundup. Modern vehicles and horseback riders guide sheep down the mountain through the valley of Maelifellsdalur. Rounding up the sheep from the high country at the end of summer is truly a community effort.

06 The center of the *rett* is the hub where sheep are sorted. Each of the outwardly radiating sections belongs to individual farms. The corral design of the *rett* dates back over 300 years. *Retts* made of materials like weathered stone, metal, and wood can be seen all over Iceland.

06

07

walk between pens, take photos, and socialize over coffee and treats. Following on horseback, farmers guide their sheep back to the farms, where the final sorting occurs. Sheep round-ups take place all throughout September, followed by horse round-ups and celebrations such as tug of war across a river, a community rét-tir dance, and traditional music in the rett.

With the first gentle snowfall in October, the northern lights dance overhead and locals begin to count down the 300-odd days until next year's community roundup. This timeless ritual feels especially meaningful today against the backdrop of a changing climate. A shared desire to connect to the land and build resilience through sustainable practices finds renewed meaning and gathers these communities in Iceland together, year after year, around their beloved sheep.

TRANSHUMANZA, ITALY

In central Italy, the age-old practice of moving livestock from summer to winter pastures is known as transhumance. It's built around the *tratturi,* ancient grass-covered routes crossed by herds and flocks for centuries, tracing the area's main trade network.

Along with livestock, artisan knowledge and customs traveled along the tratturi. Most of the routes have been erased or partially destroyed by the expansion of agricultural land, but the tradition still survives in central and southern Italian regions like Puglia, Abruzzo, Basilicata, and Molise. Like lines on a face, these ancient paths mark the age and character of the rural civilization.

During summer months, Domenico di Falco, the last shepherd of the Majella Massif in Abruzzo, lives in a

cave without electricity or running water. Wolves are a real threat to his flock on the mountains, so he only ventures down to the valley with his mules once a week to give his wife the cheese produced in his cave—it is intended for sale.

Giovanni Colavecchio, born in 1943, is a traditional craftsman of knives and scissors, and learned his profession as a child. He still recalls the Old World transhumance of the flocks and the blades-and-knives trade connected to it. Until the 1960s in Frosolone, a small town in Molise located along the tratturi, there were more than 100 artisan shops that forged steel onsite. Today producers simplify the process by using ready-made foils, considerably reducing the charm of the construction process.

On January 17 (the feast day of Sant'Antonio Abate, protector of animals) a carnival troupe of villagers ≫

08 The Colantuono are the only remaining family in Italy to observe the ancient tradition of the transhumance along the *tratturi* network.

08

dressed as cows and bulls, representing transhumance, marches before a church dedicated to the saint. The "herd" performs the traditional three laps after having been blessed following Holy Mass, in order to be able to return to the village. The participants wear bright costumes: in the crowd, a cow mask beams under a wide-brimmed hat covered with a headscarf and veil, richly decorated with long multicolored ribbons descending to the wearer's ankles; the costume's tights are also decorated with brightly colored ribbons or foulards. Each mask in the crowd has a cowbell, and the symphony of sounds is an ode to centuries of culture, labor, and interdependence.

The recent candidacy of transhumance for the UNESCO designation of "Intangible Cultural Heritage" represents a significant step toward the protection and re-discovery of this hidden Italy and of the fascinating historical legacy built into the paths and land itself.

09 A volunteer prepares the Sant'Angelo fireworks show in honor of Saint Michael the Archangel, protector of shepherds.

10 Giovanni Colavecchio, a craftsman of knives and scissors who works according to Frosolone's ancient traditions, which he began learning as a child.

11 The goat and sheep flock of the agrotourist adventure "La porta dei parchi," one of the best examples of transhumance tourism worldwide.

12 Items inside a master cutler's workshop in Frosolone reveal the transhumance's deep connections to the cult of Saint Michael the Archangel.

13 A herd passing through Torella del Sannio in all its majesty.

SHEEP HERDERS

12

13

THE PARADOXI-CAL PLAN TO TURN PROFIT INTO PRESERVATION FOR SEA DUCKS

Jean Bédard, the founder of Duvetnor, turned an age-old tradition— the harvesting of eider-down—into the driving force behind the con-servation of a natural habitat. A portrait of a man with his eyes out to sea.

By mid-April, biologist Jean Bédard still hadn't witnessed the arrival of common eiders on the islands clus-tered in the Estuary of Saint Lawrence in Quebec. But the 81-year-old man had a hunch—a few were already there, and had even started laying eggs.

His conviction came from watch-ing over the common eider colonies of Lower Saint Lawrence for nearly half a century. Since the very first time he laid eyes on a sandpiper, nothing has managed to pull him away from his favorite subject: sea birds. He pursued a post-secondary degree in biology, at a time when many of his peers had their sights set on law and medicine. To his utter de-light, his studies have often brought him to coastal environments: from Southampton Island, north of Hudson Bay, to Saint Lawrence Island in Alaska's Bering Strait. ➤

His conviction comes from watching over the common eider colonies of Lower Saint Lawrence for nearly half a century.

He speaks with excitement in his voice. "Yeah, I'm really addicted! When we're confined to an island, we have to protect it as if our lives depended on it. The islands make us realize how small our planet really is, which is something people are less and less aware of in the wake of urbanization."

In 1968 Bédard, who hails from the Rivière-du-Loup area, returned to Quebec to teach. Research funding from Université Laval enabled him to study the Estuary of Saint Lawrence's wildlife and, in particular, the common eider. At the time, the sea duck was subject to heavy harvesting for commercial purposes. Eiderdown is extremely rare and offers unparalleled insulation, which boosts its market value. Its harvest is an age-old tradition. It has been practiced for about 500 years in Quebec and for about nine centuries in Iceland. Tradition aside, the practice has not always been kind to the ducks themselves.

Bédard was genuinely shocked when he first saw the devastation wreaked by down harvesters. They camped on the islands for about a week, bringing an endless stream of disruptive comings and goings. These sustained intrusions, intolerable to the female birds, made nests more vulnerable to attacks from the likes of seagulls—predators always on the alert.

Knowing that only 5 to 10 percent of ducklings manage to make it to their first flight, the biologist decided to focus on protecting nesting areas, which play a key role in the ecological balance of the massive estuary. "I realized that if the harvest was done in an intelligent way, where we also conduct scientific studies, we could generate significant income that could then be used to ensure the preservation of the birds' habitat." A bold plan for ensuring sustained conservation was born.

Thus in 1979, with a handful of biologist friends, Jean Bédard founded Société Duvetnor, a non-profit organization, and acquired the rights to collect down on several private and public islands. A few years later, with the revenues from down sales and financial support from various conservation organizations, the company managed to buy the five islands forming the Les Pèlerins archipelago, two out of the three islands in the Pot à l'Eau-de-Vie, and Île aux

03

Lièvres. Today, some 25,000 common eider couples nest in the estuary, spread out over 20-or-so islands.

Though it may seem paradoxical, the ornithologist firmly believes that if we wish to protect a territory, we need to occupy it. "The least hint of human intrusion can destroy a colony of marine animals," he explains. "We're here to manage natural habitats, but through as few interventions as possible."

With this in mind, the down harvest had to be carefully overseen, because anyone equipped with a sack and an easily obtained permit could partake. Bédard established a comprehensive protocol for respecting the eider, and Environment Canada has been rigorously applying it ever

since. "The government has become very resistant to issuing new permits, and only grants them to people who commit to investing down profits in the protection of the habitat," he adds.

The Duvetnor pickers only visit each nest once and harvest the down by hand. They take less than half and camouflage the eggs before moving on, to protect them from predators. Then, the eiderdown is carefully processed and sterilized before being exported to Europe, where it will be transformed into outdoor clothing and king-size comforters, earning up to $14,000 (€12,500) apiece. Bédard puts this all into perspective: "To start with, the down is full of ticks, fleas, waste, and excretion. It only ➤

01 Eiderdown is harvested from the ducks' nests.

02 Unprotected by down, the eggs are vulnerable to predators.

03 Bédard's conservation efforts are focused on enforcing sustainable harvesting practices.

04

05

reaches its full value once it's been through a colossal cleaning process, spanning several months."

Duvetnor does a lot more than just pick down: scientific contribution is built into its conservation mission. "We tag the birds, draw up inventories; we try to understand what causes explosive epidemics [like those of 1976, 1985, and 2002], which killed thousands of females within 24 hours. We can intervene if

invasions are wiping out indigenous plants, for example."

The organization manages an ecotourism program, which finances island preservation and also informs visitors about conservation and biodiversity. "If we don't educate, we stagnate. People who come to see us learn to discover wildlife and realize its importance," notes Bédard. Duvetnor only allows the public to access a very limited area

unfrequented by the birds, ensuring that the majority of the territory benefits from full protection.

An inn, a few cottages, and camping spaces were built on Île aux Lièvres, while a lighthouse on the Pot à l'Eau-de-Vie Islands was restored to welcome visitors. As soon as eiders and fledglings have left their nests each year, vacationers can spend time there, observe penguins and minke whales, set off on a

JEAN BÉDARD

mushroom discovery adventure, participate in guided excursions, or simply go for walks. No kayaks, no bikes, and scarce Wi-Fi. "For me, nature is a spiritual experience. You're there to be inspired by something beautiful—nature, in the wild. We see less and less of it, now that we pillage everywhere. With Duvetnor, I feel like I've done something useful."

189

PRESERVING THE TASTES OF HOME

At Candide Restaurant, chef *John Winter Russell* is concocting a blueprint for a hyperlocal, hyper-social gastronomy.

On a springlike afternoon, John Winter Russell opens the doors to Candide, the restaurant he founded in November 2015 in the basement of an old church in Griffintown, Montreal. The wooden communal tables, the open kitchen and pantry, and the chef's frank smile all give Candide its welcoming homestead feel. Around this time of day, the staff receives deliveries from local producers. Today is cheese day. The diner is up to the brim with boxes and boxes of Clos-des-roches, made with raw, organic cow's milk, from Fromagerie des Grondines. "Life is good when you can order cheese by the kilo," Russell says. His remark is disarmingly simple but infinitely revealing of his outlook.

At Candide, Russell has built a small team of talented cooks and sommeliers who serve hyperlocal, vegetable-centric cuisine. Hyperlocal: lemon, pepper, white sugar, and olive oil are all on the list of "foreign" staples that don't even make it through the front door. Fish and meat are used as garnishes—for the sake of the planet. Everything that diners find on their plates is pesticide and herbicide free. Perhaps most importantly, every single ingredient is intimately tethered to a producer from the Estuary of Saint Lawrence and the province of Quebec. There are only three exceptions: Russell's friends from his native province of Ontario will send one batch of cherries and peaches per year; his mom's friends from Nova Scotia and New Brunswick will bring seafood when they visit; and another friend from Newfoundland harvests the restaurant's salt.

Evidently, Russell sees his producers as part of the restaurant's extended family. Supporting them throughout the seasons is a daunting task, especially when Candide also strives to live up to its reputation for serving one of the brightest, freshest, and most diverse menus in the country. To achieve a year's worth of dynamic flavor profiles (and to avoid the dreadful "beets four ways" in winter), Russell and his team have to stock up on fresh ingredients between May and December, and transform them using a multitude of traditional preservation methods. As a result, no matter the season, dishes at Candide may confidently feature fresh or transformed local ingredients such as edamame, lovage, green strawberries, smoked yogurt, edible flowers, oyster mushrooms, herring, blueberries, scallops, bottarga, parsnips, fiddleheads, smelt eggs, guinea fowl, pickerel, trout lilies, plums, malted wheat—you get the idea.

As Russell delves into explanations of his salting, drying, canning, and fermenting techniques, we grasp the full complexity of his cooking operation. While he might confidently declare that "life is good," that doesn't mean it's been easy. For the past few years, Candide's ➤

190

Russell started Candide to support a community—of cooks, farmers, cheesemakers, fishermen, and wine-makers—to make the world a better place and to refuse to let the planet become a "giant ball of fire," as he says.

chef-owner has been pushing boundaries that few restaurants have even approached. By doing this, he's come up with a blueprint for a new kind of hyperlocal gastronomy.

Two springs ago, South Shore biodynamic farm Cadet Roussel produced a magnificent batch of lovage, which Russell affectionately calls "celery on steroids." (For anyone who has never tried making a lovage salad, the learning curve is brutal: this peppery perennial should only be used in very small doses.) His team was excited to receive the farm's first cut of the season. But soon after, they couldn't keep up with the batches that followed. They lacked the manpower to cook and dry it all—and were unable to find any takers for the task. So, Cadet Roussel had to let its lovage die. Months later, Russell came up with the idea of drying the leaves at the Roussel farm using its industrial dehydrator. Since then, Candide and other restaurants in the region have been able to purchase fresh, dry lovage all summer long, letting nothing go to waste.

The amount of passion Russell deploys for a single (unusual) leafy green and its producer is emblematic of the chef's radical personality and ethical values: "I wouldn't know how to do it differently. If I can make things better, I should. If I'm not trying, then I'm being a hypocrite." After all, Russell started Candide to support a community—of cooks, farmers, cheesemakers, fishermen, and winemakers—to make the world a better place and to refuse to let the planet become a "giant ball of fire," as he says. "Together, we want to prove that we were wrong to

01

192

favor economic development over the health of our communities. I could run a small restaurant with ten seats, three days a week, and make a living. But the volume of food I am able to serve at Candide positively affects people's lives—and it means a lot."

Russell is often associated with the oft-used term *social gastronomy,* due to his involvement with the community kitchens created by famous Italian chef Massimo Bottura in Europe and South America (for that matter, he is currently working toward opening one of his own), and to his contributions to local food banks here in Montreal. But after speaking to him, it's easy to see that in fact all of his activities are acts of social gastronomy: cooking hyperlocal, ethical food, treating his staff with so much care, collaborating closely with producers, inviting guest chefs into his kitchen to share their perspectives. In a very Dalai Lama-esque way, he says: "If we put intention into our smallest actions and repeat those infinitely, ➤

04

we can solve 80 percent of the world's biggest problems. Personally, I'm already picturing the next 4,000 steps ahead!"

Before we leave the premises, Russell returns from his kitchen with a chunk of honeycomb from Miels d'Anicet, the renegade beekeepers from Ferme-Neuve in northern Quebec. He carves out a hearty spoonful of golden honey. The flowery, sugary, and waxy succulence of a single bite is bliss on the taste buds. This is how every meal ends at Candide, with the smallest of gestures filled with the greatest potential.

Summer Preserved: Examples of Candide's Signature Preserved Foods

04 Candide's impressive stores of preserves make it a role model when it comes to sustainable local eating.

CANNED TOMATOES AND BERRIES

Throughout the summer, when producers are harvesting more berries and tomatoes than the restaurant can handle, Russell and his team buy what they need for the entire year and get busy canning and stacking their pantry with jars of fruit pulp and cherry tomatoes, which will bring acidity to their dishes months later.

DRIED STRAWBERRIES

During strawberry season, Russell splits the fruit into two batches. The first is dried, and the second is juiced. The fruit juice is poured over the dried strawberries, giving them a bright, pleasant intensity and a gummy texture. This is used to garnish dishes while avoiding refined sugars.

MARINATED FLOWERS, CONES, AND ONIONS

Candide marinates and pickles various ingredients to various degrees: the staff salt flower buds and fruits, such as capers (with 10 percent salt); they pickle onions in cheese whey; and they souse larch cones in white vinegar to get larch vinegar and pickled cones.

SALTED AND DRIED SMELT

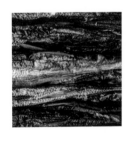

Smelt is only caught twice a year. Candide has found a creative way to serve it to their customers, who can sometimes be reluctant to try the small bony fish. The team salt it and dry it as soon as it arrives. Once it's on the menu, it's rehydrated in water, emulsified, and served with canned garlic flowers. Like anchovies in a sauce, the smelt is often used to bring out the briney, salty qualities of a dish—similar to umami.

FERMENTED RASPBERRY SEEDS AND CHILIS

Even if it's trendy, Russell warns that in some cases fermentation can mask the complexity of ingredients. Yet it can also bring out interesting flavors. He likes to ferment raspberry seeds and chilis in vinegar, with 3 percent salt. He stirs the mixture every day until it turns into a spicy condiment. His go-to pepper is the Habanada, a new hybrid type that tastes like a sweet habanero. (It's harvested, of course, by his friend's mother.)

Enduring *Artisanal Artifacts* that represent the true value of craftsmanship—and have stood the test of time

Chicago meeting of the National Association of Rudimental Drummers, the organization set out 26 essential rudiments for mastering the instrument, including the five-stroke roll, the flam paradiddle, and the triple ratamacue. In 1984, the Percussive Arts Society contributed 14 extra rudiments. Together, they make up the commonly accepted list of 40 International Snare Drum Rudiments, which is still the standard set taught today.

DRUM

Before there was language, there were sounds. Rings, chimes, tolls, clangs—nature's vernacular reverberated between animals and humans across the land. A desire to differentiate ourselves from monkeys (who also use drumming sounds to communicate) meant that we started to sing, which led to us developing words that gave shape to the rhythm of our tongues.

The cadence of our voices, of course, required an accompanying drum. As early as 6000 BC, bones that formerly banged against rocks began to strike stretched animal skin instead, with the first drum of this variety made from alligator skin in China. Around the same time, similar instruments were being invented throughout the world; despite the lack of international connection, tribes all over used them for entertainment and sacrifice, official performances, and communal gatherings.

The extended leather of the drumhead—the part that makes the instrument resonate—places it as a membranophone in the Hornbostel-Sachs musical classification system. Drums are the oldest instruments found in recorded history, with some traditional versions like the *timpani* or *djembe* so valuable to our history that they have made their way into museums as well as concert halls. The bellicose tone of these instruments has also made them official instruments of armies and military brigades worldwide, marking the rhythm at which troops should advance or retreat—from a safe distance. Bangs travel far.

Drums come in many different shapes and sizes, depending on their origin or cultural role, and each with a sound of its own. Their most significant contribution to humanity is that of music and the different genres in which drums are essential, such as jazz, rock and roll, and Latin American music, where the snare drum provides melodies with a much-needed punch.

Instruction has been essential to the development of the instrument's musical characteristics. At the 1933

PIPE

Smoking pipes was once the norm. Starting in the sixteenth century, these fashionable accessories rapidly became popular in the Western world, and still are to some extent, despite the advent of cigarettes. The practice was taken from Native American cultures who consider the tobacco plant to be holy and consume it during special celebrations, including the closing of social contracts and securing of peace treaties.

Made from ivory, ebony or other durable wood, stone, and even bone, pipes were at home in the pockets of sailors and statesmen alike—an essential tool when it came to both long voyages and briefer social gatherings. In Asia, similar devices had long been used to consume different medicinal plants, but they were usually reserved for the higher and clerical classes as a ritualistic endeavor, which became even more the case when opium began to be burned instead of eaten, as had previously been customary.

In Africa, gourds and even large tree seeds were carved to represent folk tales and used to smoke hemp; in the Congo, for example, there were entire cults dedicated to burning it to connect with the spiritual world. Similar pipes have also been found in Egypt and India: in the latter, those adept at honoring Shiva, called

sadhus or holy men, still smoke ganja frequently using hollowed-out fruit—a direct pathway to the divine. Famous writers and creatives in later centuries used them when seeking inspiration (Mark Twain and Virginia Woolf were avid smokers, for example), and some politicians, like Winston Churchill, became icons pictured with their pipe in hand, a gesture that imbued them with a kind of intellectual or statesmanlike grandeur.

Although tobacco corporations eventually saw more profit potential in rolling the leaves into cigarettes, sprinkling on a bunch of toxic additives, and selling them by the pack, smoking pipes has never truly disappeared. It might seem odd and old-fashioned to see someone packing one with dried leaves and puffing away like Popeye, but the sight of a teenager ripping a bong or a model smoking a vape pen isn't that uncommon, so why not? As the contraption has evolved, however, we seem to have lost the spiritual connection that tobacco brings, which is cherished by Native Americans, considering it as a quick nicotine fix rather than a plant to open the mind and soul.

BASKET

When doing groceries or shopping, we're now presented with a plethora of packaging options: plastic bags, compostable ones, paper options, or the more environmentally friendly tote bags. We take putting our supplies and purchases into a sack for granted, but it was once an issue that drove our species to encourage craftspeople to ponder upon it deeply and innovate. Before indestructible and bio-degradable containers alike became omnipresent, humans relied on baskets to accumulate, store, and transport products from one place to another.

In the past, the process behind making one of these receptacles involved weaving or sewing organic materials such as straw made from tree bark, vines, animal skin, or grass, plying and bending the fibers into geometric forms that corresponded to their use. Indigenous communities in Asia historically opted for rattan, which is quite durable, while in the Americas wicker has long been used to store cereals and grains. In Europe, baskets made of willow were once standard, with water hyacinth also a key basket material, whereas in Africa the primary material was raffia palm, often bedazzled with colorful ceramic beads (with Zulu and Wolof baskets being particularly intricate examples).

From the purely utilitarian to the decorative, baskets have long played an important role in both commerce and trade as well as folk ceremonies, honoring gods with their content (usually fresh food, crafts, or flowers). Around the world, each tribe or group has its own pattern, with some even representing entire legends and folk tales. Despite the regional variations, these essential community objects can be apportioned into four categories depending on the weaving technique: coiled, plaited, twined, and splinted.

The oldest surviving examples of these items, from ancient Egypt, are 12,000 years old and were unearthed at the Faiyum settlement. The organic nature of ancient baskets' components makes it difficult to find complete samples, but more recent remains have been uncovered by archeologists researching Middle Eastern, South American, and other Old World societies who used baskets in their daily interactions as a lighter replacement for more robust pottery and ceramics. No matter where—or when—you traveled around the world, it seems, there would be—and continues to be—some kind of bag or basket waiting to help you transport back whatever you were to find there.

CHAIR

Chances are, while you're reading this piece, you'll be sitting on some type of chair. Whether it is an ill-suited stool, a comfy recliner, or a stylish Chandigarh chair designed by Pierre Jeanneret and Le Corbusier, this piece of furniture is omnipresent around the world. We take them for granted whenever we're feeling tired; ➤

197

we seek their support to help us work or study; we need them to traverse the globe, whether by air, land, or sea. But for a long time, they weren't even in the picture.

Up until the sixteenth century, most people relied on chests or benches to rest upon, although thrones and early versions of chairs—reserved for religion and royalty—date back to early settlements, where the first hominids who wanted more than a place to put their backsides added backrests to stones and blocks of wood, with legs being a later addition. Rulers back then didn't have many budgetary restrictions; pharaoh chairs, for example, were made of ebony and ivory, and bedazzled with fine metals and precious stones.

More than just a decorative object, chairs were the literal seat of power, which commoners could only dream of occupying. The oldest known chairs originate in Asia, and are depicted in ceremonial paintings from the sixth century. In later times, Europeans reserved them for blue-blooded families, until the Renaissance got into full swing and woodworking became commonplace, allowing families to adorn their abodes with similar seating. When revolutions began to take place, the social ones saw chairs fly out the windows of castles and manors, while the industrial variety allowed for them to start being mass produced, making them easily obtainable.

In the modern era, the chair became a favored mode of expression for architects, artists, and designers. Charles Eames dominated the lounge scene, while Salvador Dalí turned it into a masterpiece (with stilettos and all)—some were named after animals (peacock) and others after cities (Acapulco). They've been shaped like eggs, hands, and disco balls split in half, and put in bedrooms, kitchens, and living rooms alike. Some even give massages, while others come with matching footstools.

For a brief moment, the office workforce's desire for something less sedentary presented a threat to chairmakers, when standing desks and exercise balls briefly came into fashion to replace the humble and utilitarian chair. It was worth a try, but exercising turned out to be more effective in keeping idle employees healthy, and the chair regained its place of prominence in the office. Ultimately, despite changing trends and our need to stay mobile, it seems this versatile piece of furniture won't be going out of fashion any time soon.

SHOVEL

There's something so inherently natural about the act of digging that almost all creatures do it—whether grow or hide food, set traps, or make burrows for shelter. Humans are no exception. When the first communities began to settle and build villages, a desire for efficiency meant that work that was once done manually had to be taken to another level. Cue the shovel.

The "invention" was actually more of an accidental discovery; during the Neolithic era, our predecessors realized that bones, specifically the shoulder blades of beasts, could be turned into spades that removed more soil than any set of hands that operated them ever would. Eventually, when more precision was required for the purposes of agriculture and construction, a handle was added.

During the Bronze and Iron Ages, the shaft remained, but the bone was replaced with a sharper, more robust component: metal. Later on, when populations and settlements started to grow and become cities and then metropolises, shovels were replaced by heavy machinery powered by hydraulic systems, rendering manual labor obsolete (when it came to rapid growth).

Despite the evolution of the digging implement from bone to excavator, shovels never disappeared. In fact, they're easily found at any local hardware store, having become more ergonomic and sturdy, with sharper blades and more comfortable handles making them easier to operate.

One of the oldest commercial shovel makers has been operating for nearly 250 years: founded in 1774 by army captain John Ames in Massachusetts, his eponymous company specializes in construction tools. According to the organization, it was thanks to Ames's steelmaking abilities that the

United States managed to grow rapidly through mining, infrastructure development, and industrialization. Its oldest shovel, from 1784, remains in the archival collection of Stonehill College in Easton, Massachusetts.

MASON JAR

Agriculture developed out of the need to accumulate enough provisions to keep entire communities alive and well fed. As processes improved and became more efficient, the year's crops presented a surplus; bountiful harvests offered the opportunity to save food for leaner times through different preservation methods, including pickling. Such a technique required a gadget that allowed the user to control the process while keeping the ingredients locked airtight.

Several methods utilizing mud jugs, buried boxes, and pickle packs had been in use since antiquity, but it was not until the mid-nineteenth century that the process was made more affordable and accessible. In 1858, John Landis Mason, a tinsmith, invented his eponymous receptacle whose patented screw-on lid kept it hermetically sealed, minimizing the possibility of food rotting. (We also have him to thank for designing the first screw-top salt shaker, but that's a different story.)

Mason's method, which quickly became the standard way to conserve food, involves leaving some space between the food and the neck of the jar, avoiding any overflow. This allows a rubber-seal lid to be placed on the top, with a screw-on band set over it before the jar is sterilized in boiling water. Then, the lid is tightened and the jar is left to cool down at room temperature, creating an impermeable vacuum that seals the content.

Before commercial canning became commonplace, these kinds of jars were omnipresent in kitchens

around the world, only to be relegated to old cupboards and storage basements for years, until the nostalgia for vintage objects and bygone eras helped them make a comeback.

Nowadays, they go hand-in-hand with detox juices, amateur pickling projects, and DIY trinkets that fill them up to the brim, having become repositories of a new wave of traditions. One brand in particular, the Ball Corporation, stands out from the rest. Initially specializing in selling only hand-blown jars, the company's vessels are now mass produced in Broomfield, Colorado, where it has since diversified its portfolio to include the development of aerospace technologies, although it continues to manufacture the product once created to perfect the preservation techniques initiated by the French chef Nicolas Appert, known as the "father of canning."

TEAPOT

Few objects possess as much of a ceremonial quality as the teapot. With a straightforward appearance and made of basic materials—steel, clay, glass—its design takes advantage of the laws of thermodynamics and physics, maximizing its steeping power to quench the thirst and offer

a pick-me-up to its users, a task it has been fulfilling since the days of the Yuan dynasty. As Kublai Khan conquered modern-day China, his need for a warm refreshment on the go was quickly solved by master craftsmen, who devised an elegant and efficient way to replace the boiling cauldrons previously used, without the need of a brush to stir the brew.

We know about the early days of the teapot in Asia through written history, and the oldest surviving physical specimen dates back to 1513. This antique spouter now lives at the Flagstaff House Museum of Teaware, where it shares the space with similar artifacts from around the world, including several models that were found in Europe, a result of the tea trade of the seventeenth century. These ones were made of porcelain and glazed blue and white, a design commonly associated with Chinese decor—there were no porcelain kilns in the Old Continent at the time, which is why sipping tea was reserved for the higher echelons of society. This exclusivity came to a halt in the early eighteenth century, when ceramist Ehrenfried Walther von Tschirnhaus developed the hardpaste Meissen porcelain that soon became popular throughout the region.

Outside Asia, the British are also very heavy tea drinkers, which may be due to William Pitt the Younger, a prime minister who cut the tax on tea after a bad crop increased the price of the raw ingredients for ale, at that point the most popular beverage on the isles. Supply and demand only grew more with the East India Company's trade with China and India, with tea eventually also making it to colonial America, where elaborate teapots were made out of silver, particularly in Boston. Similar pots, made of copper and other metals, were also being used in northern Africa and India, where mint ➤

concoctions and spice-infused teas are still commonly drunk to this day.

Tea has been served in royal court (Queen Elizabeth is a big fan and hosts tea parties at Buckingham Palace every year), in Buddhist Zen ceremonies (matcha is said to be sacred), as a cold drink to stay refreshed through the summer (if mixed with lemonade, it's officially known as an Arnold Palmer, in honor of the golfer), and to bleary-eyed shift workers worldwide. It's estimated that there are more than 3,000 varieties of tea found throughout the world, but no matter how many combinations you might want to seep, the teapot will, in essence, always remain the same.

SWISS ARMY KNIFE

A Swiss Army knife is a memorable tool; its bright red cover—marked with Switzerland's coat of arms—invites users to pick it up and unfurl its many contrivances, one by one, discovering a new possibility with each new gizmo. The sense of amazement is a civilian outcome of what was initially developed as a war accessory, a device that would allow soldiers to pry open even the toughest food cans as well as assemble (or disassemble) their rifles.

Toward the end of the nineteenth century, every soldier in the Helvetian military was given a folding pocket knife, named the Modell 1890 (despite being officially released a year later). The knife's first iteration had a wood casing, a blade, can opener, reamer, and screwdriver. Despite its iconic country-branded name, the first 15,000 knives were in fact assembled in Solingen, Germany, a fact that made Karl Elsener uncomfortable. The Swiss cutler set out to make sure that future army recruits would have a knife made in the country they fought for.

Competing against the Germans, Elsener risked it all. On the verge of bankruptcy but rich in commitment, he decided to incorporate a spring mechanism that eased the tool's rotation. The new model impressed everyone except the Swiss Army, who didn't commission it. Regardless, his invention—patriotically branded with a white cross emblem—sold successfully and allowed Elsener's company (originally named Victoria, after his mother; later Victorinox) to become prosperous again. Elsener was not without competition, however. A fellow cutler, the vehement Francophone opponent Paul Boéchat, marketed a similar contraption, attracting the

attention of the Wenger Company, who would ultimately take over knife production for the Swiss military.

The companies began a duel—a commercial one, that is—that would twist and turn in the years to come, starting with the Swiss government split commissioning both companies to supply the tools. The decades-long battle finally ended in 2005, when Victorinox struck the final blow and acquired Wenger, with the Wenger brand subsumed by Victorinox in 2013, making the stainless victor the single provisioner of the soldiery. As of 2008, 50,000 new knives rest in infantry pockets each year, with many thousand more in those of the public.

SANDALS

Humans must have walked thousands of miles before they decided their primate soles had evolved to become too delicate to continue without some extra padding. Perhaps it was when they got to higher altitudes that the sharpness of rocks and cool burn of snow was too much to handle. Maybe it was the harshness of the sizzling deserts that scorched their feet to the point that a layer between them and the ground had to be invented.

Given the evidence, the second scenario seems to be the most likely, with the oldest pair of sandals ever found—10,000-year-old sagebrush bark footwear—discovered in Oregon's arid landscape, specifically Fort Rock Cave. In ancient Egypt, some 5,000 years later, sandals were protecting the feet of the pharaohs and their entourages, while shoeless slaves built pyramids and palaces they would never set foot in. During Roman occupation, sandals were almost fully democratized (the Greek word *sandálion* and turned into *sandalium,* resulting in the word's current iteration), with foot soldiers

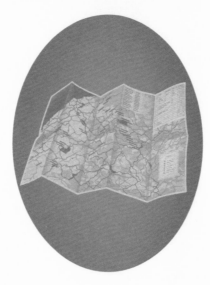

known to wear *caliga*, made from leather and hobnails.

Up until the seventh century, showing one's toes was commonplace, but when the Christians dictated that displaying them was considered vulgar, sandals were left to the clergy and lowest classes, social groups that weren't financially capable of being on-trend. Mostly made from natural fibers, leaves, or wool, over time the footwear would see new and different variants built using a range of materials, even including tire rubber in the case of the Vietnamese *dép lõp*. Despite such resourcefulness, most of the world's sandal producers ultimately opted for plastic as a raw material, unknowingly making it one of the main future ocean polluters.

Despite the many changes to both society and fashion over the centuries, the first-ever shoe has stayed rooted in human culture. Sandals continue to be widely used in developing nations and warmer climates, with many different versions available, from vegan leather to fur covered, toe loop to slingback. As of late, those made from recycled or organic materials are in vogue; versions such as the Mexican huaraches, which were once seen as being solely for the underprivileged who couldn't afford fully covered shoes, are now making a comeback—wrapped around the feet of hipsters and millennials who appreciate craftsmanship.

MAPS

Before humans moved on from the nomadic lifestyle, there weren't any real borders that delimited nations. But with the first settlements came the subsequent need to establish boundaries, which emphasized land occupancy and ownership.

Although cartography was widely used in the cradle of civilization—places like Babylon, China, and Greece—the first maps to have been discovered date back to 14,500 BC, and, instead of featuring the world, they highlight stars. Illustrations of the Pleiades and the Corona Borealis were found in Lascaux and Cueva del Castillo, respectively.

Used as navigational and geo-referencing tools, maps became paramount as empires grew, tracing commercial routes for the Romans and the Turkish, for example, as well as the vast extent of their territorial possessions. Centuries later, as the European conquerors sought to expand their reach—and that of their religion—cartographic centers (most notably the Majorcan school, which produced the Catalan Atlas) were launched to create guides featuring new routes and the virgin frontiers of the New World.

Wars and expansion were the main reasons that the world was put on paper—first as a flat Earth, then as a three-dimensional globe after Ferdinand Magellan and Juan Sebastián Elcano successfully circumnavigated it—allowing us to understand our position on the planet at any given time. Technological breakthroughs such as lithography and later satellite imagery have been crucial in making maps more precise and accessible, so much so we all now carry one in our pockets and most likely use it more than once a day.

That said, Earth is extensive and some of it still remains uncharted, with the Amazon, several mountain ranges, and—most notably—the oceans too vast and impenetrable to be outlined; for now, their grandiosity keeps them off the charts.

THE REBIRTH OF SAKE

A new generation of Japanese brewers is remaking sake by returning to traditional brewing methods while pushing boundaries

During the postwar years of the 1950s and 1960s, sake—the ancient brewed rice beverage of Japan—was rough liquor that could curl your hair. Wartime shortages had compromised the quality of rice as well as the brewing techniques used, and to stretch out their product, makers added distilled alcohol and sometimes even artificial flavorings. Despite the drop in quality, this fortified sake remained a salve for emotional wounds. "People needed strong medicine, because it was a very hard time for Japan," recalls Masumi Nakano, the fourth-generation head of Dewazakura Sake Brewery in Japan's northern Yamagata Prefecture.

But by the late 1960s, with the onset of the Japanese "economic ➤

miracle" and a dramatic rise in household incomes, consumers were eager to buy prestige foreign wine and spirits. Sake was quickly becoming passé.

Instead of folding, as thousands of sake breweries were to do in the ensuing years, Nakano and his team of brewers got to work on a new brew that was to change the sake world forever. In 1980, after five years of tinkering, Dewazakura issued the world's first mass-market ginjo sake, called "Ōka," or "cherry blossom," to reference the elegant aromas of Japan's revered national symbol. It was a much more refined, delicate, and aromatic brew than what Japan had become used to, made with highly polished rice and fermented at unusually low temperatures. It had none of the rough, hangover-inducing qualities of the mass-produced sake of the day.

Since its founding in 1892, Dewazakura has always been driven by technical innovation. Nakano says, "we challenged ourselves to create an affordable version of ginjo," the category of ultra-refined "competition sakes" that breweries pour all their skill into each year. The goal was to win awards and bragging rights with a few special-edition bottles. The idea of mass marketing these unicorn sakes—which require hours of rice polishing and carefully tended koji (mold-inoculated rice) starters—was unthinkable; they were far too expensive and time-consuming to make.

Nakano and his team of brewing experts consulted with a variety of craftspeople, ranging from carpenters and electricians to machinists and experts in refrigeration technology, to create temperature-controlling jackets that keep fermentation tanks at suitably low temperatures. The brewery invested in a fleet of refrigerators to preserve its delicate brew in mint condition until its pasteurization and bottling.

When it was finally released, Ōka was embraced by both locals and sake fans across Japan, setting off a worldwide "ginjo boom." Today, the word "ginjo" and its many subclassifications—junmai ginjo, daiginjo, junmai daiginjo, and tokubetsu junmai ginjo—are shorthand for a premium class of sake that continues to create new fans around the world.

A YOUNG BREWERY HEIR RETURNS HOME

In October 2000—20 years after Ōka's debut—Tomonobu Mitobe, another son of Yamagata, was living his dream in Tokyo, working in export and risk management for a large international trading company. He had grown up a 15-minute walk from Dewazakura, at his family's Mitobe Brewery, though with no interest in taking over the family business. ➤

01

02

THE REBIRTH OF SAKE

03 Brewery worker Jun Yuuki savors the sweet chestnut-like aroma of mold-innoculated koji rice.

04 Yamagata Masamune sake made with Omachi rice (left) and Dewasansan rice (right).

05 Charms from Matsuo Taisha Shrine in Kyoto, where the goddess of sake is enshrined.

04

03

01 *Moromi,* or "main mash," tanks at Mitobe Brewery, where the bulk of the company's sake fermentation occurs every winter.

02 A snow-covered Mitobe Brewery in February.

05

The decision was swift and easy. He headed back to Yamagata.

Although the ginjo boom had taken off internationally, domestic sake sales were still dropping. Before making any changes at the brewery, Mitobe took time off to travel the world, then toured his home region with a renowned brewing expert from the prefecture's sake research institute. Mitobe realized the road to profitability lay in premium ginjo sake rather than in the more run-of-the-mill honjōzo sake (which is cut with a small amount of brewers' alcohol to enhance the sake's aroma) that his family's brewery was turning out for the local market.

He saw how heavy, rich styles were giving way to fresher, cleaner sakes, and spotted a way for his brewery to inject a sense of local terroir into its sake. While Dewazakura's water was on the soft side, the mineral-rich hard water that percolated down from the nearby Ōu Mountains that Mitobe Brewery used had the potential to make a sake that was strong, defined, and full bodied.

In the 20 years that have intervened since Mitobe's return home, the Yamagata Masamune brand has become revered around the world for just this type of sake. It's an example of how Mitobe and a whole new generation of brewery heirs are remaking sake into something that both sticks to traditional brewing methods and pushes boundaries, resulting in a kind of deliciousness that would have baffled and amazed their ancestors in equal measure. The makers are embracing a return to ancient jizake (local, handcrafted) styles, using slower, more labor-intensive methods of brewing and locally grown rice—and often even local wild yeasts and koji-kin, the aspergillus oryzae mold needed to convert rice's starch to sugar so that fermentation can begin. ➤➤

06 Freshly steamed rice being lifted from the steamer at Dewazakura Sake Brewery.

07 Rice being added to the starter tanks at Dewazakura.

Then, four years into his job, he got a call from his father, who told him that the brewery, founded in 1898, was in crisis: would he come back to help out? The son replied by asking, "What will happen if I don't come back?" The reply: "After you get married, can you send one of your kids?" Neither Mitobe nor his sister were yet married. "My father had never forced me to do anything in my life," Mitobe recalls.

THE REBIRTH OF SAKE

08

08 Mats laid out in preparation for the cooling of freshly steamed rice.

09 Left to right: Dewazakura Ōka Ginjo, Ichiro Junmai Daiginjo, and Dewa Sansan Junmai Ginjo.

10 Stirring the starter tank.

09

10

THE REBIRTH OF SAKE

13

14

11 The exterior of Banjo Brewery in Nagoya, Aichi Prefecture.

12 The tatami-matted Kuheiji family home, which is over 200 years old.

13 An ancient abacus and a scale for weighing gold are reminders of an earlier time.

14 Entrance to the Kuheiji home.

15 Kuheiji (top row, second from right) and his brewery team.

15

16 Kuheiji ages his premium junmai daiginjo in French oak barrels.

17 The entryway to Banjo Brewery is decorated with a *noren*, a short curtain usually hung over shop entrances.

18

19

20

Mitobe is also a symbol of the new generation of sake brewery owners who fill the role of both president and master brewer. For centuries, the role of master brewer, or *tōji,* was out-sourced to seasonal workers who farmed or fished during the summer off-season. Another aspect of this new style of sake brewing is a return to locally grown rice. Earlier premium ginjo makers transported rice from farther afield to make the best sake. But Mitobe cultivates 21 acres of his own sake rice, mainly local varieties suited to the cold climate such as Dewa Sansan and Yuki Megami, and even a local table rice called Kame no O, emulating the domaine-style vignerons of France who grow and ferment their own grapes. Rice, Mitobe says, "is a very symbolic product in Japan, and consumption is decreasing." He sees his role in part as being someone to absorb and keep alive some of that generational knowledge.

ADOPTING FRENCH IDEAS OF TERROIR

One president-brewer who is at the fore-front of this terroir-driven approach to sake making is Kuno Kuheiji, the fifteenth-generation head of Banjo Brewery in Nagoya. Just as Van Gogh, painting in the South of France, injected elements of Japanese woodblock prints into his work, Kuheiji says he has brought inspiration from French domaine-style wine making to bear on his sake making in Japan. He was the first, for example, to put vintages, that is, the brewing year, on his elegant wine-like Eu de Désir.

He has also de-automated Banjo's entire brewery and gone back to hand-made techniques, hired a Frenchman to help him brew, and employed a Japanese farmer to tend his rice fields in neighboring Hyōgo Prefecture. "If we don't raise our own rice, we're only telling half the story," he says.

Sitting in his more than 200-year-old tatami-matted family home, dotted with artifacts of another age—a worn wooden abacus, sliding paper shōji screen doors, and an ancient metal scale used for weighing gold—Kuheiji muses on future plans. One day he'd like to set up a brewery in Hyōgo, so there is no distance between the field and the brewery. His ultimate goal, he says, "is to capture the drama of the rice field in the bottle."

It's an ancient idea made new again, one of many that is keeping the art and craft of sake making alive. Sake has captured the imagination of an ever-widening international market, but the more important question remains: can it recapture the love of Japan's ever-fickle domestic consumers?

18 Inspecting the freshly made mold-inoculated koji rice.

19 Sampling junmai daiginjo straight from the barrel.

20 Kuheiji's wine-like Eau du Désir vintage sake expresses "the drama of the rice fields."

A BETTER FUTURE THREADED TO THE PAST

How *Bergthora Gudnadóttir* and *Jóel Pálsson* launched Farmers Market-Iceland and helped revive the tradition of designing sustainable clothing.

In 2005 designers Bergthora Gudnadóttir and her husband, Jóel Pálsson, did something revolutionary in the design world—they waged war with the fast-fashion giants. For years, global brands like H&M expanded their empire by trading tradition, culture, and craftsmanship for profit. Feeling inspired to take action against the titans, Gudnadóttir and Pálsson launched Farmers Market-Iceland, a sustainable design company and clothing brand that proudly weaves Icelandic heritage and traditions into chic modern concepts. The company focuses on sustainability, community, and the use of natural fabrics in stylish collections that channel the distinctive essence and history of classic Nordic country living.

Building the Farmers Market brand was a natural fit for the duo, who have strong ties to the Icelandic design and art scene. Gudnadóttir studied fashion at the Art Academy of Iceland and then immediately started working in the fashion industry in textiles. Pálsson is a professional jazz saxophonist and composes with various Icelandic musicians. Coming up in the art scene in Iceland together, they felt a deep connection to the traditions and customs of their home and to how it shaped their cultural identity.

The Farmers Market mission statement nicely sums up Gudnadóttir and Pálsson's beliefs and design practices. "We wanted to place ourselves at a junction. A place where heritage meets modernity, the national meets the international, and where the countryside meets the city."

They started with a modernized line of *lopapeysa*, knit wool sweaters that have been staples for Icelandic fishermen and farmers for generations. When imports of mass-produced clothing first arrived in Iceland in the early 1900s, knitting the sweaters became a symbol of resistance and pride. This coincided with a rising boom in knitting fashions from other parts of Scandinavia through the influence of magazines. As the popularity of knitting the homespun ➤

01 Strandir, in
Iceland's rural
Westfjords
region.

02 Icelandic
horses at the
base of Hekla,
an active
volcano.

03 Camping
in the cool
Icelandic
summer with
woolens to keep
warm.

03

sweaters grew over time, they became emblematic of Icelandic cultural identity. The Farmers Market lines of modern *lopapeysa* extend the curious tradition of knitting as protest and are beautiful symbols of the brand's beliefs in practice.

The modern sweater designs incorporate new materials and silhouettes in thoughtful ways to evolve traditions with care. Classic Icelandic knit workwear uses the rough and heavy wool cultivated from local sheep. This dense and coarse material is perfect for workers exposed to the severe weather conditions of the countryside, as it naturally prevents moisture from reaching the skin. But the powerful insulation proved too much for those living and working in cities and climates less severe than the Icelandic countryside. So Farmers Market developed subtle, precise adjustments for a more contemporary fit along with a thinner design using a blend of heavier local wool and lighter, softer imports. This evolved design approach blends the icon of heritage with light refinements to help accommodate modern living in global cities. Sourcing exact materials from international suppliers with a sustainable design ethos was challenging, but it is an important pillar for how the brand operates.

According to Pálsson, "a good part of the wool we use is Icelandic, but we also carefully source ➤

woolen yarn from Scotland, merino wool from Australia, recycled yarns from Italy, waxed cotton fabrics from British Millerain, and silk." Using this mixture of natural materials from all over the world and local textiles, Farmers Market is able to sustain traditions and meet global needs.

Over the years its collections have expanded to include knit outerwear, woven pants, shirts, dresses, and a broad range of accessories. Farmers Market is sold to devoted fans in over 50 stores globally. "The clothing is very popular in Japan, where our pieces are styled with other modern clothing. It makes us really happy to see someone from another culture appreciate and embrace ours. It's a really nice feeling." Even with the consistent growth and popularity, Farmers Market remains a small, privately owned operation, and they plan to stay that way. "We want to continue finding new partners and good producers with sustainable practices. We like that by doing so, we are helping put pressure on the big companies to change and to be better."

The fast-fashion giants have taken notice. Since the launch of Farmers Market, which has helped popularize the idea of sustainable design methods, global retailers have started shifting their practices, improving their supply chains and making commitments to better practices overall. Even the worst offender of all, H&M, has since stated they will use 100 percent recycled or sustainable materials by 2030. For Bergthora Gudnadóttir and Jóel Pálsson, running Farmers Market will always be about "creating beautiful products with the highest ethical standards toward humans and nature." This happy husband and wife with a passion for good design are making the future more sustainable by honoring the traditions of the past.

04 The modern *lopapeysa* wool knit sweater worn on the beautiful Snaefellsnes peninsula.

05 Gudnadóttir working with a technician on an Icelandic wool blanket in a local knitting factory.

06 Farmers Market's classic Nordic-style sweater made of undyed wool.

06

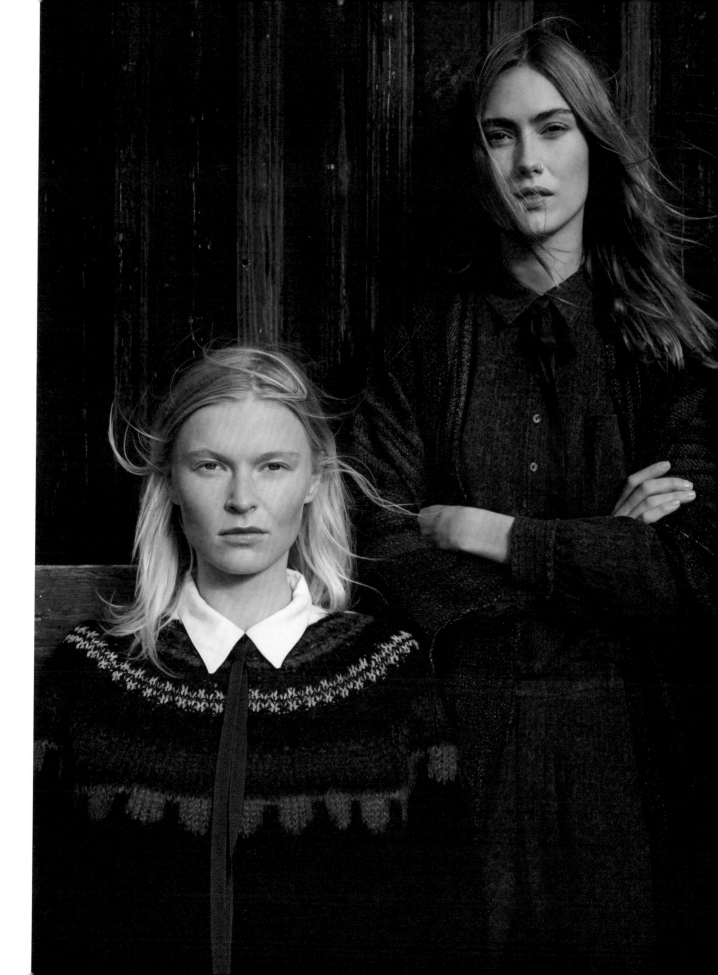

MINIMAL BUT PURPOSEFUL: DESIGNING STRUCTURES IN NATURE

In Norway, *Tormod Amundsen* and his team design "invisible" architecture: carefully crafted, environmentally integrated small shelters that must blend into and be absorbed by their reworked earthly surroundings.

"*Bios* is life, *topos* is place," says birder and architect Tormod Amundsen of Biotope. The Greek words that combine to form his firm's name also reflect the team's viewpoint as architects in the wild.

"A key aspect of my background is the Norwegian concept of *bålkos,*" Amundsen explains. "All you need is an outdoor ireplace—*bål*—and the time and comfort to enjoy it. I spent countless days and nights in nature, often building a temporary shelter for the night. My goal is to create the ultimate *bålkos* conditions."

Biotope did just that when it moved its offices to the arctic town of Vardø in an effort to help rebuild the local economy there. In 2009, Vardø was ranked as the worst town in Norway financially, yet Amundsen saw an opportunity to turn that around through avitourism (birdwatching). The firm's work has always been a manifestation of its passion for the natural world of flight.

With a mission to inform both local inhabitants and tourists from abroad about the area's biodiversity, Biotope has designed and built open ➤

220

02

03

and inviting structures that help create closer connections to nature. Whether through nature trail development, cultural space planning, birdwatching towers, photo hide buildings, or even by producing books, Biotope sees architecture as a powerful tool for protecting and promoting birds, wildlife, and nature.

So let's talk about that architecture. How does Amundsen wield that tool? "After all, people will protect and care for what they learn to appreciate," he says.

For one, his photo hides and weather shelters are designed with the landscape in mind. The sightlines play off the character of each location, taking into account wildlife and wind direction. Balance between human comfort, aesthetics, and a sensitivity to the needs of birds is essential. "The way we build expresses our views of people and nature," says Amundsen.

A standard bird hide is basically just a wooden box pierced with holes or windows for viewing or photographing wildlife. It's essentially designed to hide people away from birds while allowing them fairly

close access. From an architectural standpoint, photo hides might tend to be drab or intrusive, and to suggest to occupants that they do not belong there—that they need to hide from nature.

Architecture is so commonly regarded as an end goal in itself—one the Biotope team feels is problematic, outdated, and pompous. But they

see new generations of architects valuing a more purposeful approach, and striving to be a part of positive change, even if that means seeking inspiration outside of educational institutions. It might be known as climate-adapted architecture or eco-conscious design, but it's still in its infancy. People must now consider climate change when designing ➤

01 The Kongsfjord cliff cabin: a small retreat open to the public year-round, situated on the very edge of a 100-foot (30-meter) precipice overlooking the Arctic Ocean.

02 The nature shelter in Varangerbotn. A small communal building with a fireplace inside, it is often used by local schoolchildren.

03 Biotope's designs are open and inviting, while accounting for the needs of wildlife and unique character of each location

04 The northern wind shelter in Vardø, built with local slow-growth pine sourced from the south side of the Varangerfjord.

Biotope sees architecture as a powerful tool for protecting and promoting birds, wildlife, and nature.

buildings, making them adaptable to rising sea levels and salinity, as well as to violent weather surges, or better yet, integrating them into their surrounding environments.

According to Amundsen, whenever architecture projects refer to the environment, they typically only calculate levels of CO$_2$ emissions. This isn't unimportant, but it's a very narrow vision of the relationship a building has to the nature it dwells in. "Going into nature with a science approach did not appeal that much to me," he explains. "I wanted to connect with nature on a more emotional level, not at strictly a numerical level of science."

Harkening back to the pursuit of balance in how buildings interact with their environments, ultimately in many cases less is more. Amundsen emphasizes that "when designing, we often ask ourselves *how little is enough?*" A key characteristic of Biotope's designs is that they have to be open and inviting. They should make one feel sheltered, connected, and focused on visible wildlife, as well as on the nature surrounding it. They should be there, but not.

05

06

05 Auroras dancing over the Kongsfjord cliff cabin.

06 Interior view from the Kongsfjord cliff cabin, looking north over the Barents Sea.

07 The king eider, an Arctic dweller and iconic species of the north, breeds in Siberia and winters in Varanger in large numbers.

08 King and common eiders in the waters around the island of Vardø, seen here from the Steilnes nature shelter. Flocks of tens of thousands of eiders gather in these rich waters for winter.

08

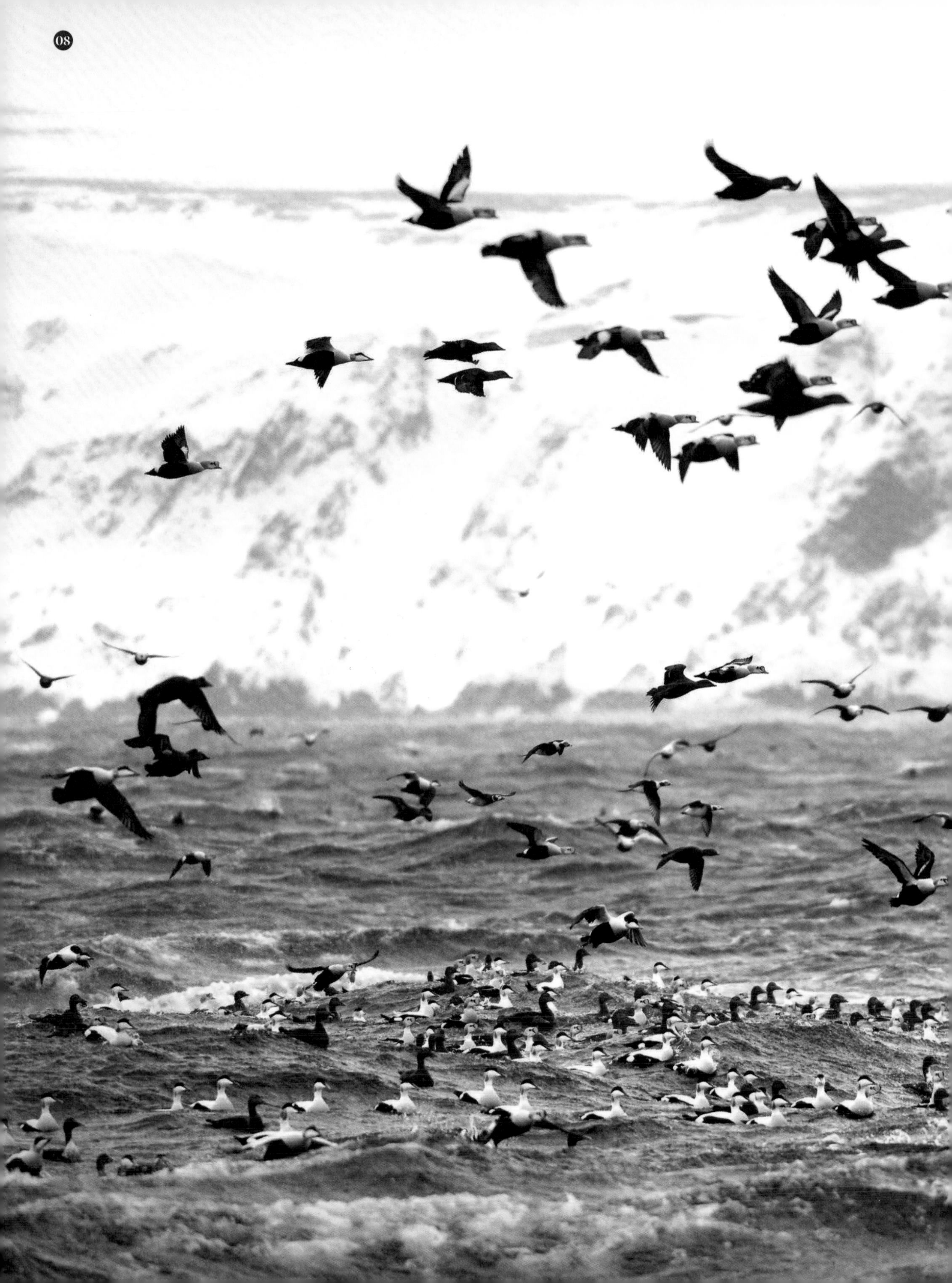

SAUNA SPIRITS

Saunas aren't just places to visit on vacation. In the world's most sauna-rich cultures, they're everyday sites of immense social and spiritual importance, not least because they feel divine.

Thinking about the past tends to conjure images of hardship, struggle, and scarcity. But it's worth remembering that some of our oldest and most long-standing traditions are designed around relaxation and self-care. For centuries, humans have invested a lot of thought and intention in the experience of feeling warm together, by the fireside, inside an igloo, and at no time is this more evident than when sweating it out in a sauna. Some cultures even consider saunas to be sacred places, even if in certain cases they're an **01** everyday affair. ➤

229

01 Mooska smoke sauna in Võrumaa, Estonia.

02 Lämpimänä sauna's icy swimming hole at Luonetjärvi lake near Tikkakoski, Finland.

03 Three men go ice swimming in Vuorilampi lake after a sauna in Jyväskylä, Finland.

04 A man takes a post-sauna dip in the freezing water of Vuorilampi lake.

02

FINLAND

For the last two years, Finland has been named the happiest country in the world, and the Finns attribute this to a lifestyle firmly rooted in nature. Getting outside is so essential to the national identity that its been enshrined in legislation. Thanks to a law called "everyman's right," people are allowed to roam wherever they want—on any property, no matter who owns it. But even if Finns love the nature that surrounds them, the harsh weather conditions and never-ending darkness during winter make it tough love. To thrive and get through it, Finns draw on their sense of *sisu,* a term that connotes grit and resilience. That, and saunas.

Finland has more saunas per capita than anywhere in the world. The country boasts 3.3 million saunas for just 5.5 million people. Every family has one. That's because saunas are traditionally built into most homes, doing double duty as a place to unwind and as a heating device for entire houses. And saunas aren't just a private affair. Brave Finns regularly gather in small groups to match their sauna sessions with icy swims. Proponents say that after a good sweat in the sauna, taking a dip in a frozen lake not only feels amazing, but it's good for your health too. Aches, pains, even depression: none can withstand the invigorating effects of a frosty post-sauna plunge.

ESTONIA

While the rest of the world is grappling with the massive digital shift transforming societies, the small Eastern European country of Estonia just went ahead and did it. After gaining independence from the Soviet Union in 1991, it set about rebuilding its whole economy on a foundation of tech-forward, digital-first policies. Despite living in the most ➤ 04

technologically savvy nation on Earth, Estonians maintain a deep connection to their traditions. During the severe winters, when temperatures can easily dip to -40 °F/C°, foremost among these traditions is the smoke sauna.

Most saunas are heated with wood fire, but Estonian saunas have no chimney, so the smoke is trapped in the room until the stones reach about 212 °F (100 °C), when it is finally vented out and the sauna-goer can enter. The tremendous heat sterilizes the surfaces, which is why they were traditionally used as birthing rooms and viewed as places to clean both body and soul.

Estonian smoke saunas have been added to UNESCO's Representative List of the Intangible Cultural Heritage of Humanity. Often undertaken with the whole family, a typical session lasts three to five hours and takes the form of a purification ritual, encompassing drumming and singing. Sauna visitors are whipped gently (and not so gently) with branches to whisk off dead skin and stimulate circulation. The saunas are typically built beside ponds—chilly in summer, frozen in winter—that draw dry-roasted sauna-goers in need of a cooling plunge. Then it's back inside for another round. Cook. Rinse. Repeat.

The sense of being baked alive is reinforced by the presence of hanging strips of beef or wild game, which are smoked over the course of the session and then consumed at the end, perhaps while checking emails. In Estonia, connecting with tradition never has to mean going without a good internet connection.

JAPAN

The Japanese take shorter vacations—only two or three days at a time, usually—but they maximize their restorative potential, especially with visits to hot-spring spas called *onsens*. Japan is a volcanically active country, so there's no shortage of geothermally heated springs: more than 30,000 of them are scattered throughout the country's 3,000 onsen towns. The oldest of these, Dōgo Onsen, is believed to be more than 3,000 years old. The earliest onsens were the domain of the wealthy elite,

but they later evolved into a widely popular and accessible form of relaxation and self-care. Today, onsen culture continues to evolve, especially as it has become more popular with tourists. For example, in the past, both genders bathed nude together at an onsen, but gender segregation is now common.Nudity is required, modesty, however, is encouraged. If you're into ink, check before you travel. As of 2015, about half of all onsens forbid guests with tattoos, a practice designed to exclude members of Yakuza gangs. The onsens are slowly opening up to skin art though, as tattoos are becoming more globally ubiquitous.

Onsens are prized for the different minerals they contain—these can be identified by the color of the water. Red means iron, milky means sulfur. There are 19 naturally occurring chemical elements associated with hot springs, each conferring some particular benefit to the person who soaks in it, and to be considered an onsen, the spring must contain at least one of them. In Ibusuki, spa-goers bury themselves under hot black mineral-rich sediment from the nearby Kaimondake volcano and then go for a soak in the springs. The water at onsens must be hot: 77 °F (25 °C) is the minimum for government-certified onsens, but 122 °F (50 °C) is not unusual. Spa-goers don't only visit onsens for the mineral-rich water either. Many are located in nature, and bathing in a quiet forest atmosphere or beautiful natural environment is also a part of the experience.

05 Visitors take a sand bath in Ibusuki, Kagoshima Prefecture, Japan.

06 Mariann and Henry Liimal go for a dip in a pond beside a smoke sauna with their son, Kaius, and daughter, Lovise, along with the sauna's proprietor, Eda Veeroja.

BUILDING A NEW WEST WHERE HUMANS, LIVE-STOCK, AND PREDATORS CAN CO-EXIST

In rural Montana, *Malou Anderson-Ramirez* works to support thriving and diverse wildlife populations, sustain ranching businesses, and ensure a wild and healthy ecosystem for humans and predators alike.

In a rugged southwestern corner of Montana, 2.2 million acres of otherworldly blue geysers, dramatic canyons, and rich archaeological sites are protected within the boundaries of Yellowstone National Park. Were it not for the popularity of the northern gates of this vast ecosystem, the Tom Miner Basin might be overlooked entirely. A lone dirt road bisects the valley: a bowl of grasslands that, to a casual observer, might simply appear as a sweeping patchwork of cattle ranches. But these sage- and aspen-covered hillsides are the setting for a decades-old conflict. Home to at least two packs of wolves and one of the densest populations of grizzly bears in the Lower 48 states, this is ground zero for a controversial convergence of predators and prey, humans and livestock. ➤

236

At the center of this ever-evolving struggle is Malou Anderson-Ramirez, a third-generation cattle rancher, mother, and outspoken leader in the movement for coexistence—the art of sharing the landscape with threatened meat eaters like bears and wolves. Hers is a multi-generational story of old customs and modern tools, of antiquated mindsets and the evolution of a new doctrine for existing in a shared ecosystem.

To Anderson-Ramirez, the legacy of conflict between ranchers, predators, and conservationists is divisive and polarizing, yet she's hopeful that conversations and strategies will shift, as she insists they must. Tom Miner Basin is just a fragment of the larger story of protecting what natural resources still exist on the planet.

THE RISE OF PREDATOR TOURISM

Over the last decade, the remoteness that once deterred outsiders has brought to the basin new visitors hoping to spot a large predator in its home environment. On any given day around sunset at this time of year, tourists congregate with binoculars and expensive cameras in hand. It's a flurry of car exhaust and desperation for the chance to see the much-maligned grizzly in the wild—from a safe distance, of course. Recently, as she was driving to the hillside, Anderson-Ramirez heard a collective gasp among onlookers. Two massive creatures appeared on the ridgeline and came bumbling toward the fence, stopping occasionally to dig at the red-tinged caraway root that brought them to the pasture. "If they had a mother, they'd know not to come this close," says Anderson-Ramirez. "We have hunters' packing pistols and not bear spray, and that's why we have twin bear cubs without a mother. They'll probably get shot too." Camera shutters clicked in a cacophony of noise as they disappeared into the sunset, oblivious to the unfolding story that will ultimately determine their fate.

KEEPERS OF A NEW WEST

Anderson-Ramirez's grandfather came to Montana after the Second World War. As part of a Midwestern **01** family who'd made its living in steel, he was captivated by the West's rugged beauty and eventually moved his growing family to the Tom Miner Basin in 1959. A well-educated outsider, he had to work to gain the approval of the community. "We've always sort of been the rogue ones in this valley, but well respected. My grandfather had an open mind and had to make friends because he had to learn how to ranch. He learned to be a good neighbor."

Today, Anderson-Ramirez, her husband, Dre, and her two daughters are the only members of her family living full-time on the 1,600-acre property, caring for the livestock year-**02** round. As agriculture has become ➤

03

01 Tiny homes built by Dre Anderson-Ramirez, Malou's husband, welcome tourists from spring until late fall.

02 Malou Anderson-Ramirez took on the responsibility for her family's ranch and its long history.

03 The Tom Miner Basin is a gorgeous and delicate ecosystem.

04 Electrified fences are only a small part of the coexistence solution.

04

05

less financially stable, they've had to turn to tourism to pay the bills. Two tiny homes (built by Dre) and a beautifully restored stone schoolhouse welcome Airbnb guests to the property from spring until late fall. The shift in economics here is indicative of what most western rural areas are experiencing: an evolution from the "Old West," with an economy based on farming, ranching, and resource extraction, to the "New West," which relies heavily on tourism, recreation, and technology.

06

A NEW ETHICS OF COEXISTENCE

Up until ten years ago, the Anderson family followed conventional ranching techniques. Wanting to restore grassland and manage livestock differently, Anderson-Ramirez began a program through the Savory Institute called "Holistic Management." One technique called "low-stress livestock handling" encourages cattle to behave more like the bison that once grazed these lands and knew how to guard their young against predators. For Anderson-Ramirez, the program was a revelation. "This could change the entire ecosystem," she thought. The challenge was to find a way to implement these tactics and unite a community with vastly different perspectives. According to Anderson-Ramirez, it's deeply complicated. "Here we are trying to coexist with animals in this landscape and we can't even coexist with each other. That's the other story of Tom Miner Basin."

Together with sister-in-law Hilary, Anderson-Ramirez co-founded the Tom Miner Basin Association, which

07

Hers is a multi-generational story of old customs and modern tools, of antiquated mindsets and the evolution of a new doctrine for existing in a shared ecosystem.

works on a number of fronts to support thriving and diverse wildlife populations, sustain ranching businesses, and ensure a wild and healthy ecosystem. She was also recognized by the National Geographic Chasing Genius committee for a vision that she believes could potentially revolutionize the way ranchers and predators coexist. Her idea is to insert a tiny microchip into each of the animals in a herd to monitor their health and whereabouts. If one becomes injured or killed, the GPS technology would allow a rancher to find it and tend to its wounds, or record how it died. Since ranchers receive compensation from the government for losses due to predation, this ➤

system works in their favor, allowing them to quickly and easily document casualties. As Anderson-Ramirez explains, "We want to keep the wilderness intact and cattle ranching alive." Her many strategies inspire a new ethic: to confront the errors in old ways and to respect all of the inhabitants of this land, not only those that serve and feed us directly.

08 Anderson-Ramirez's daughters will grow up knowing the delicate balance between life and death that exists in the basin.

08

BACK TO THE FUTURE

For the Incas, time had a circular structure: the past, present, and future influenced each other continuously. This idea became the foundation for Mater Iniciativa, the agricultural and culinary laboratory headed by *Malena Martínez and her brother Virgilio*, the internationally renowned Peruvian chef.

Nestled in the hollow of a mountain in Moray, to the northwest of Cusco, are the remains of the most famous Inca terraces in Peru. An amphitheater surrounded by wilderness at first sight, it reveals an ingenious agricultural laboratory.

Like bleachers, the platforms follow the natural slope of the rock. Stones placed skillfully at the edges hold the earth in place. These store heat during the day and release it into the soil at night. Although the platforms are only a few feet apart, the temperature varies significantly from one level to the next. This creates microclimates, which allowed the Inca people to cultivate a wide array of plants in the best possible conditions.

More than an architectural chef d'oeuvre, the circular terraces are a perfect illustration of Incan ingenuity. They remind us of the importance of observing the nature that surrounds us, and of working with ancestral species that are naturally adapted to their immediate living environment. Because in the Incan worldview, the past, just like the future, is alive in every present moment.

VERTICAL TERROIR

In Peru, as elsewhere in the world, we are observing a cultural return to the values of an agricultural system in which all living organisms exist in symbiosis—a balance between the principles of biodynamics, permaculture, and regenerative agriculture. Mater Iniciativa has been using this approach in all of its research projects since its inception.

Created in Lima in 2013, the agricultural and culinary laboratory headed by Malena and Virgilio Martínez aims primarily to expand knowledge of Peruvian ecosystems. Discoveries are then integrated into Virgilio's flagship restaurant, Central, named the sixth best restaurant in the world in 2019 by The World's 50 Best Restaurants. Each of a ➤

244

single meal's 16 courses, called "moments," showcases food from a distinct altitudinal environment—a particularly delectable way of exemplifying the benefits of vertical (rather than horizontal) farming.

The first "moment," for example, originates 40 feet (12 meters) below sea level, highlighting fauna and flora off the coast of Lima. Sargassum, in particular, is found in abundance on nearby beaches. The brown seaweed is distinctly unpopular among sunbathers, but it provides a living environment for a multitude of species, such as seahorses, octopuses, and an impressive number of fish. Placing sargassum on the dining table is an act of gratitude for the essential role it plays in the balance of marine life.

Some "moments" proudly emphasize a dish's ingredients (such as hyperlocal tubers and the famous coca leaf) as well as the rich diversity of the region's environments. Dishes are served with historical awareness—centuries of priceless Peruvian traditions in each ingredient.

"WE SHARE EVERYTHING"

In early 2018, the team behind Mater Iniciativa opened their newest restaurant, Mil, in Moray. It pays homage to the particular richness of Peru's high-altitude ecosystems. "It's a challenge to concentrate solely on local ingredients," says Luis David Valderrama, chef of the establishment. He must constantly communicate with his suppliers, who contribute actively to the design and development of Valderrama's creations.

To promote the transmission of ancestral knowledge, the team at Mater Iniciativa turns to the inhabitants of the neighboring villages of Mullak'as-Misminay and Kacllaraccay. Like many Peruvian communities, these villages carry on Incan agricultural

01 Virgilio Martínez pictured at the Andean restaurant Mil with his sister Malena (left) and wife Pia Léon (right).

02 The menu at Mil consists of eight courses named after the ecosystem that inspired them.

03 Several fermented plants that will be added to dishes and cocktails at Mil.

04 Corncobs of different colors and sizes spread out on the large worktable.

03

04

traditions, though the empire collapsed nearly 500 years ago.

"We listen to the communities, try to understand how they see their world, and what they wish for in their lives," says Rodrigo Cabrera, coordinator of Mater Iniciativa, Mil, and Central, the polestar restaurant of the Martínez siblings in Lima.

Mil's herbarium is a fitting example of this exchange—a slow and magnificent co-creation that sits inside a small earthen structure, which also houses the restaurant and laboratory. Drying plants are hung from long strings, the way we might hang works of art (here, the objects are considered as works of memory).

Corn cobs of various colors and sizes are spread out on the large work table. Petri dishes hold clearly labeled groups of kernels, as though we were in a scientific research lab. There are also dozens of potatoes and other tubers that are specific to Peruvian culinary culture.

In addition to studying all of these plants, the team at Mater Iniciativa grows various species on its 17 acres, and thus the lab supplies some of the food for the menu at Mil.

In their wish to include the two neighboring communities in their entire process, the Mater Iniciativa team called on anthropologist Francesco D'Angelo. He spent ➤➤

05 Drying plants hang from long strings, like works of art.

06 The first "moment" (course) at Mil.

07 Various plants grown at Mater Iniciativa feature on the menu at Mil.

08 The herbarium is a vessel for the transmission of ancestral knowledge.

09 Inside, the Mil is modest and earthy.

09

time among these communities learning their dynamics and customs. "We are building a horizontal relationship, and we think this contributes to lasting human relationships," D'Angelo says. The inhabitants had their doubts about Mater Iniciativa's intentions at first, given that it is the organization behind one of the best restaurants in the world. But little by little, the team has gained the trust of the villagers, who now collaborate with the organization in both the fields and the kitchen. "In addition to being paid for their labor, workers get to take home half of what's harvested,"

We are observing a cultural return to the values of an agricultural system in which all living organisms exist in symbiosis.

MALENA AND VIRGILIO MARTÍNEZ

10 Restaurant Mil is located in the heart of the historical Inca terraces in the Andes.

11 Mater Iniciativa has a catalog of ingredients to maximize knowledge transmission.

12 In the lab, Virgilio talks about various species of corn, tubers, and other plants.

13 Nothing is imported here; every single ingredient is local.

D'Angelo says. "They don't work for us, they work for themselves, and for the project."

Mater Iniciativa now has a catalog of ingredients to maximize knowledge transmission. The organization has also created a menu for Mil that honors farmers and pickers in the Cusco area. Farmers from other regions of Peru provide the ingredients for the other three restaurants in Lima.

THE MORE-THAN-PRESENT MOMENT

If the present urges us to delve into our traditions and revive forgotten practices, it's clearly because we're in search of meaning. To remedy our situation, here and now, we must recognize the preciousness of nature, food, and the people who bring them together to feed us. Like the Incas, let us draw from our past and begin to see the present moment as a chance to approach one another, to create a more sane world, a world that's truly human.

COME TO THE TABLE, RETURN TO THE SOURCE

Jim Denevan, the creator of Outstanding in the Field—which brings the entire dinner table to the farm—wants to make you a little uncomfortable (and give your food a lot more meaning).

Last June, on a dock in Tuna Harbor, San Diego, a local fisherman stood and addressed a single long dinner table, with place settings for more than 200 guests. On their plates were the fruits of his labor, sourced from the waters in front of them: poached spot prawn, rockfish ceviche, and cured halibut balanced with arugula from a local farm. The diners looked out over the wharf, where the fisherman had worked, down the elegantly set table that ran the length of the dock and out to the sea beyond.

"In his late 60s, this gentleman got up and spoke about his entire life working on the sea," said Jim Denevan, whose company, Outstanding in the Field, had organized the waterside meal that evening. "This is the guy who caught the fish, and there it is on the table. And when he tells his story," Denevan continued, "I'm blown away by the beauty of people's lived experience of providing food for people."

Today, most of us do not come from large families, live on farms, or eat, in our regular domestic lives, dishes whose components are harvested by the same people with whom we share our meals. And yet, food-based events like this dockside meal in San Diego—slow, at the source—feel familiar to us; they feel essential. This is partly true due to the work and vision of Jim Denevan.

More than 30 years ago, while Denevan was touring France and Italy working as a model, he noticed how much more integrated food was into daily and local culture than what he was used to in America, where industrialized agriculture and marketing had all but erased the human connections to what eventually ended up on dinner plates. At home, groceries were cheap, available in bulk, microwaveable, disposable—the opposite of *slow*, at every stage.

When he returned to California, he wanted to be a part of changing the increasingly distant relationship Americans had with their food. "It was really strong in my head," said Denevan. "I really wanted to see how the world would be better in terms of food."

In 1999, at age 37, Denevan came up with the initial concept for Outstanding in the Field: why ➤

01 Oustanding in the Field founder and land artist Jim Denevan performs one of his large spirals at Secret Sea Cove, north of Santa Cruz, CA.

02 Outstanding in the Field's team prepares to serve the table at Stinson Beach, CA.

03 Jim Denevan, creator of Outstanding in the Field.

bring the farm to the table when you can bring the entire table to the field where the food was grown, then share it—and the stories behind it—with a large dinner party?

The geography that inspired Denevan's idea—and the location of one of the very first Outstanding meals—was his brother Bill Denevan's organic fruit farm, located near a redwood forest with heirloom apple trees overlooking the Pacific Ocean. In year one, Denevan's team hosted three meals on California farms. Since then, his company has grown considerably. Following the same guiding principles, Jim and his team have produced more than 1,000 events, in all 50 states, and in 15 countries. His long, recognizable dinner table has been set at the foot of Mount Fuji, among agave plants at a mezcal distillery in Oaxaca, and on the cliffs of Big Sur.

This is impressive, but even more so when you consider that Denevan started Outstanding during *pre-internet America*. At that time, people didn't see the value of sitting together at communal tables and sharing family-style platters with people ➤

JIM DENEVAN

04 Hidden just blocks from Hollywood Boulevard, Wattles Farm was the venue for an entirely plant-based event.

05 At Peeler Farms in Texas, the family have been raising wagyu beef and lamb for over a century.

06 The farm-to-table experience at Ayers Creek Farm in Gaston, Oregon.

07 Outstanding in the Field visited a vineyard straddling the border of Napa and Sonoma Valley in California's wine country.

JIM DENEVAN

they didn't know. "People were like, 'I don't want to break bread with a stranger and pass a platter around to a little group around a farm,'" said Denevan. Outstanding was not just a novel food experience. It was, as one of Denevan's curator friends would call it, an "intervention." It didn't just exist in culture—it confronted it head-on.

To strangers, in the early days of Outstanding, this approach to doing business appeared questionable. Denevan and his team took their first trip to Canada in 2005. Upon arriving at the border, even the guards questioned their sanity. "That sounds like a terrible idea," Denevan recounted the border guard saying. "Why would you want to put a table on a farm? There are flies and it's hot and windy." He forged ahead though, because he was Jim; the world just needed a little time to catch up with his vision, he thought. And he was right.

Several years later, when he returned to Canada, the guards had a different reaction. "They were like, 'Oh, I know what that is, I've seen pictures, it looks great, have a great trip!'" Outstanding went from losing money at every event to selling out almost every meal. As social media began to play a huge role in Denevan's publicity efforts, local celebrity chefs eventually signed on. Nowadays, each and every event is so well supported, he said, that they're all easily able to live up to the name on the flyer: Outstanding.

For Denevan, it's not just about the excellence of the food or the connections forged between guests and farmers and chefs that ➤

The diners looked out over the wharf, where the fisherman had worked, down the elegantly set table that ran the length of the dock and out to the sea beyond.

make any of his events feel memorable —though all of that is crucial. For him, it's also about that ephemeral, natural element of a lived experience, how everything can suddenly change in a moment, outside of our control, that makes every event singularly special.

The celebration of the moment is something he learned to embrace in the earlier days of Outstanding, while at a meal on a vegetable farm in Craftsbury, Vermont. He placed his table right in the middle of a field of fiery buckwheat, which, Denevan noted giddily, was exactly the same height as his table. The site was too far away from the barn, which **08** might have provided shelter in the case of rain; sure enough, the skies opened up and poured warm drops on Denevan's guests. Everyone was soaked. "It rained the entire event, all the way through," he recalled. "There was a salad that became soup." But he noticed something incredible: his guests were still having a good time. Some came up and told him afterward that it was the best event they had ever been to.

If you end up near one of the vegetable farms, fruit orchards, olive groves, date gardens, or beaches where yet another Outstanding event will soon be taking place, you might consider stopping by. Reconnecting with nature and food, and the people who produce it, is a powerful ritual—especially when the moment takes over the plan. "When people are brave and willing to get out of their typical patterns," said Denevan, "they're rewarded, they're fulfilled by it." He will set the table. All you have to do is put on some field-friendly shoes and find your way to it.

08 The dockside dining experience at Stock Island, Florida paid homage to the local seafood and maritime tradition.

09 The summit of California's Mount Tamalpais provided no shortage of dramatic vistas for a particularly memorable edition.

JIM DENEVAN

263

INDEX

THE NEW TRADITIONAL

HERITAGE, CRAFTSMANSHIP, AND LOCAL IDENTITY

This book was conceived by BESIDE and edited and designed by gestalten.

Contributing editors: Catherine Métayer, Casey Beal, Mark Mann, and Jeremy Young for BESIDE
Edited by Robert Klanten and Maria-Elisabeth Niebius for gestalten

Introduction by Catherine Métayer for BESIDE

Editorial management by
Lars Pietzschmann for gestalten

Photo curation by Eliane Cadieux for BESIDE
and Madeline Dudley-Yates for gestalten

Design, layout and cover by
Jonas Herfurth for gestalten

Illustrations by Dawid Ryski

Typefaces: Stanley by Ludovic Balland,
Proza Display by Jasper de Waard

Cover images by Ari Magg (top left), Camrin Dengel (top right), Gustavo Vivanco (bottom left), and Eric Hevesy (bottom right)

Printed by Printer Trento S.r.l., Trento, Italy
Made in Europe

Published by gestalten, Berlin 2020
ISBN 978-3-89955-984-2

For more information, and to order books, please visit www.gestalten.com

BESIDE
beside.media

Bibliographic information published by the Deutsche Nationalbibliothek. The Deutsche Nationalbibliothek lists this publication in the Deutsche Nationalbibliografie; detailed bibliographic data is available online at www.dnb.de

None of the content in this book was published in exchange for payment by commercial parties or designers; gestalten selected all included work based solely on its artistic merit.

This book was printed on paper certified according to the standards of the FSC®.

FSC MIX Paper from responsible sources FSC® C015829